new
force
on the
left

new force on the left

Tom Hayden and the Campaign Against Corporate America

John H. Bunzel

Hoover Institution Press
Stanford University, Stanford, California

Acknowledgment for permission to reprint:

By Tom Findley. From "Tom Hayden: Rolling Stone Interview, Part I."

By Straight Arrow Publishers, Inc. © 1972. All Rights Reserved. Reprinted by Permission.

From Joel Kotkin, "Tom Hayden's Manifest Destiny." First published in *Esquire* (May 1980).

From Justin Raimundo, "Inside the CED," *Reason*, February 1982.

Hoover Press Publication 280

Library of Congress Cataloging in Publication Data

Bunzel, John H., 1924–
  New force on the left.

  Includes bibliographical references.
    1. Radicalism—United States.   2. Hayden, Tom.
3. Radicals—United States—Biography.   I. Title.
HN90.R3B78 1983   322.4'4'0924   82-21323
ISBN 0-8179-7802-X

Manufactured in the United States of America

Design by P. Kelley Baker

contents

preface

the 1980 presidential election left the Democrats foundering in a wave of reaction against the Carter presidency and a party that had lost touch with the electorate. In 1981, the resistance that congressional Democrats raised against President Reagan's economic policies failed. Whatever the fate of the Republican administration's programs, Democrats must revitalize their basic philosophy if they hope to regain the support of the voters. Even if the economy does not revive, Americans are unlikely to endorse the resurrection of programs that failed in the past. If the Republicans succeed, the Democrats will have to wage political battles not only on the issue of economic stewardship but on others as well. In short, the way will be open for new leaders capable of inspiring Democrats to a reorientation toward new goals.

Tom Hayden, who last November won election to the California State Assembly, aspires to be one of those new leaders, and Economic Democracy, his program for saving the country, represents a radical departure from mainstream Democratic and Republican economic proposals. Economic Democracy is designed to give the public direct control of large corporations and to institute a "new moralism" that would turn Americans toward more personal, inner-directed values rather than material wealth. To Hayden, this new approach is more "legitimate" because the people, rather than corporate executives, would have the major say in economic decisions. Everyone would be content in leading a more "conserving, caring and disciplined lifestyle." [1]

Hayden's credentials as a reformer of American society are of a special kind. He was a founder of Students for a Democratic Society, took part in numerous student uprisings, and was a defendant in the 1969 Chicago 7 conspiracy trial. He organized blacks in the ghetto of Newark and revolutionaries in the hills of Berkeley. In the 1970s he campaigned to get the United States out of Vietnam and himself into the U.S. Senate. Today, he is building a political machine, the California Campaign for Economic Democracy (CED), with his own considerable energy and talent and wife Jane Fonda's considerable income.

Although Hayden has gone through a variety of political phases, there are definite patterns that run throughout his career. Sam Hurst, staff director for CED, finds "an almost eerie similarity between the Port Huron Statement which founded SDS and his [CED] essay on the crisis of liberalism . . . I think you'll find an enormous consistency in

Tom that very few people have really thoroughly examined."[2] This consistency provides insight into Hayden as well as his plans to change the Democratic party and the United States itself.

Hayden has always taken a highly moralizing attitude toward the lack of "legitimacy" in the American political and economic order, demanding (among other things) the immediate restructuring of the country to expand "participatory democracy" and help enrich the "human spirit." Convinced that his plan will reverse the country's decline in moral health and democratic vigor, Hayden seeks to pull the "grass roots" away from the Republicans and lead the people and the Democratic party into a new era. But Tom Hayden wants more than a successful political career. He wants and intends to make history.

Both Tom Hayden and I were in Chicago in August 1968. I was a delegate from California to the Democratic National Convention, where many long days of tough debate were devoted to trying to hold a faction-ridden party together so that Richard Nixon would not become president. Hayden was a leader of the radicals engaged in a violent confrontation with the city's police. In the opinion of many observers, their activities in Chicago contributed to Mr. Nixon's election. I had followed Hayden's career since the early 1960s, but the events of the summer of 1968 served to focus my attention on the New Left and to deepen my interest in Tom Hayden. Most leaders of the political left who fought against "the system" have since become part of it—and are largely forgotten. Tom Hayden has also "gone straight" (as a radical wag once put it), but he is not forgotten. I have chosen to focus on his ideas and activities because he represents a wider trend of thought and is a paradigm for those of the radicals of the 1960s who have remained politically active.

* * * *

I am in debt to several people who helped in the writing of this book. While a senior at Stanford, John Hansen worked closely with me in chronicling the history of Hayden's career and in pouring over his writings and speeches. James Scaminaci III, a Stanford graduate student in sociology, also researched different phases of Hayden's career and provided important political insights. The assistance of both Hansen and Scaminaci was invaluable. Thanks also go to many at the Hoover Institution for their encouragement, particularly Robert Hessen, a colleague and friend, who read the manuscript and gave me the kind of criticism that an author needs (even when it hurts) but does not always get. I cannot thank him enough.

Susan Hammond deserves special thanks for typing the manuscript again and again. It was not her fault. It was mine. "If you can't be right," she would say, "at least be careful." It finally worked. I am grateful for her patience and good cheer.

the
ghosts of
radicals
past

1

tom hayden entered the University of Michigan at Ann
Arbor in 1957. He majored in English, planning to become
either a writer or a reporter. He was indifferent to politics
until his junior year when the civil rights movement caught
his attention. On February 1, 1960, four black students ordered coffee at a "whites only" lunch counter at a Woolworth store in Greensboro, North Carolina. The anticipated
response—that the store's policy was not to serve "col-
oreds"—prompted several days of sit-ins by hundreds of additional students. In the weeks that followed, sit-ins were
held across the South (as well as in segregated cities in the
North) and became a widespread tactic of the civil rights
movement.[1] "I didn't get interested in politics at all until
after the sit-ins," Hayden was to recall.[2] In the spring of

1960, he took part in demonstrations at Woolworth stores in Ann Arbor.

At the end of the school year, Hayden was appointed editor of the *Michigan Daily*, the university student newspaper. He still was unsure about politics. "Maybe I already was a radical but then it didn't have a name. It was like trying to mimic the life of James Dean or something like that. But the other half of me was in the establishment, the ambitious young reporter who wanted to be a famous correspondent."[3]

The "beat generation" intrigued Hayden, and he was inspired to travel to California during the summer of 1960 after reading Jack Kerouac's *On the Road*, one of the primary "beat" testaments. The California trip dispelled any doubts that Hayden may have had about political activism.

When he arrived at Berkeley in June, Hayden, in order to contact local student activists, "immediately went to the first person I saw who was giving out leaflets."

> The people I stayed with in Berkeley were very involved . . . This guy, Herb Mills, came up to me one day, and I had heard that he was a leftist, and I didn't know what that was, but he drove me out to Livermore one day and showed me the nuclear reactor, where all the hydrogen bombs were made, with the fence around it, and he described the nuclear weapons and the arms race. And then another day, he drove me out into the fields and valleys, and he told me about the Chicanos and the farm workers, and the conditions under which they labor.[4]

Mills and the others with whom Hayden stayed were members of SLATE, a student political party formed in 1958 at the University of California. Fervent advocates of academic freedom and of civil rights and critics of hysterical anticommunism, SLATE members had been very successful in student government elections. In 1960, SLATE members were organizing a civil rights demonstration outside the Democratic National Convention in Los Angeles, and Hayden went with them. He spent much of his time at the convention outside on the picket line. After the convention, Hayden felt "exhilarated" by his new political awareness, writing articles back to the *Daily* "proclaiming the birth of an American student movement." [5] On his return to Ann Arbor in the fall, Tom Hayden set out to become one of the catalysts of that movement.

He arranged a showing on campus of *Operation Abolition*, a film produced by the House Un-American Activities Committee (HUAC) and narrated by J. Edgar Hoover. In May 1960, HUAC had held hearings at San Francisco city hall. Several hundred students (mostly from Berkeley) had staged a sit-in at the hall to protest the committee's fanatical anticommunism. Police using fire hoses had drenched the demonstrators and ejected them from the building. Sixty-three students were arrested. *Operation Abolition* attributed the sit-in to a communist conspiracy aimed at subverting American youth. The film became a hit on many college campuses, but for reasons other than those HUAC intended. Students identified with the demonstrators and were simultaneously amused and outraged by the committee's stodginess and intolerance. [6] To Hayden, the movie made clear that there were really outdated and irrational people on congressional committees who were behaving in, you know, insane ways, and the San Francisco police were their allies. Young people like ourselves were being washed down the stairs of City Hall, getting their heads broken. Those people were like us.[7]

Encouraged by the film's success at Michigan, Hayden formed VOICE, a group patterned after SLATE and destined to become one of the core chapters of Students for a Democratic Society (SDS).

SDS grew out of the Student League for Industrial Democracy (SLID), campus branch of the League for Industrial Democracy, a democratic socialist organization founded by Upton Sinclair, Jack London, and Clarence Darrow. Al Haber, a graduate student at Michigan, had worked with SLID in the late 1950s. Despite SLID's small membership, Haber saw the organization as a tool for stimulating the student activism that he was convinced was ready to erupt in the United States. Haber attempted to increase SLID's appeal by incorporating a broad range of issues into the group's concerns. To symbolize the group's wider interests, the handful of SLID members voted in January to change the name of the organization to Students for a Democratic Society.[8]

Haber tried to persuade Hayden that the *Daily* should support the civil rights sit-ins. In May, at an SDS conference in Ann Arbor on civil rights, Hayden met student activists from across the country as well as other leaders of the left such as Michael Harrington. That summer, while Hayden was in California, Haber moved to New York. He often returned to Michigan during the 1960–61 school year, however, to confer with Hayden on SDS's development and to travel with him to other campuses to establish local affiliates.

After graduation, Hayden attended the annual congress of the National Student Association (NSA) in the summer of 1961 with Haber and SDS activist Rennie Davis.[9] He lost a bid for national office and was turned down as a delegate to the NSA's international student conference,[10] but he made additional contacts with student activists and displayed a flair for national student politics. Afterward, Haber offered him a job as field secretary for SDS,[11] working out of an Atlanta office as liaison to the Student Non-Violent Coordinating Committee (SNCC). SNCC ("snick") had been formed in April 1960 to coordinate local black student organizations into the civil rights movement. Its members participated in the Freedom Rides of 1960 and black voter registration drives in Mississippi and elsewhere. In Albany, Georgia, Hayden was arrested with SNCC leader James Forman and two others for sitting together in a segregated train station waiting room, and in McComb, Mississippi, he was beaten up by a band of whites for participating in a voter registration drive.

SDS's reputation grew. Hayden sent reports of civil rights activities to Haber, who then mimeographed and distributed them to students across the country. As Paul Booth, later vice-president of SDS, remarked, "Tom was SDS's project and Al was SDS's office."[12] Hoping to expand SDS into a vanguard for social change, Haber called for a conference to be held in Ann Arbor in December 1961 in order to formalize the structure of SDS and clarify its goals. Haber and Hayden expected the conference to unite behind the popular civil rights issue, but the delegates' concerns were diverse. They not only were interested in civil rights, but in the cold war, the Bomb, university authoritarianism, and other issues. Hayden realized that unified action required incorporation of these issues under the common theme of dissatisfaction. At the end of the conference, he was charged with the task of drafting a manifesto that would address all of these grievances.

The Port Huron Statement, so-called because of its adoption at the SDS convention at Port Huron, Michigan, in June 1962, reflected the negativism of the group: "Although mankind desperately needs revolutionary leadership, America rests in national stalemate, its goals ambiguous and tradition-bound instead of informed and clear, its democratic system apathetic rather than 'of, by, and for the people.'" [13] The statement stressed the need for young people to become involved in politics to overcome the problems that the country had failed to surmount. Built around some of the political concepts in the New Left theory of Columbia sociologist C. Wright Mills, it was the first articulation of New Left aspirations, and it influenced thousands of students over the next several years.

Hayden still believed that with enough work and dedication the United States' flaws could be redressed through conventional political channels. If the poor and neglected could be organized into a cohesive force, the government could be made to serve the people more faithfully. Hayden saw SDS as the source of leaders for that effort. As SDS president in 1962, he launched the Economic Research and Action Project (ERAP). By organizing community-action groups in urban ghettos, SDS members tried to demonstrate to the poor that unity would enable them to take an active part in local political and economic affairs.

Hayden spent most of the next three years running the Newark Community Union Project (NCUP), the ERAP program in Newark, New Jersey.

> We would invite ourselves into homes and tell people that we wanted to help create an organization in the community, that we believed that people can solve their own problems by themselves, that we see ourselves as a resource or a help in getting people together but that we want to organize a meeting on the block in which everyone would find out— everyone would talk about what their immediate problems were and some organized form would be created that would maybe allow for the dealing with those problems.[14]

Tactics included rent strikes, demonstrations, and the submission of petitions. NCUP was the most successful of the several ERAP projects, but its victories were small—better garbage collection, a small playground, tenement repairs, and the termination of an urban renewal project that would have displaced some ghetto dwellers. Still, on the whole, the plight of poor blacks in Newark changed little.

Although his main interest in SDS was ERAP, Hayden

was "aware of Vietnam as early as '62–'63." [15] The organization planned a march on Washington to be held in the spring of 1965 in opposition to U.S. involvement in the war. With the bombing of North Vietnam in early 1965, the march, originally expected to draw perhaps two or three thousand people, grew into a demonstration of about twenty thousand. The march made SDS famous; escalation in Vietnam made it grow. Looking back, Hayden would say, "Vietnam was the immediate cause of the radicalizing of the student movement in the U.S. from '65 on." [16]

In an attempt to establish a relationship with the American peace movement, the North Vietnamese invited Herbert Aptheker of the Communist Party, U.S.A., and two companions to travel to Hanoi in December 1965. Aptheker invited Staughton Lynd, a radical historian from Yale, and Lynd in turn invited Hayden, whom he had met while working with SNCC. The three of them traveled through Prague and Peking on their way to North Vietnam, meeting with Vietnamese and local communist officials in each city. They were led through Hanoi and the surrounding countryside, visited villages and factories, talked with Vietnamese, and even met with an American POW whose plane had been shot down. After their return, Hayden and Lynd wrote *The Other Side*, an account of the trip that argued that U.S. involvement in Vietnam was both immoral and illegal. The thesis of the book was that although the American government might be at war with Vietnam, the American people were not. [17]

With the Hanoi trip, Hayden became something of a celebrity. He was concerned that conservatives would use the trip to discredit SDS and endanger the Newark project, and he hoped to return quietly to NCUP and not be troubled by the authorities. However, as journalist Jack Newfield wrote:

> When Hayden returned on January 9 [1966], he was not greeted with handcuffs and subpoenas. His passport was not even confiscated . . . Instead, he was [offered] an hour on Canadian network television, an article in the *New York Times Magazine*, an article in *Life*, appearances on the Barry Gray radio show and on Channel 13 [in New York]. A publisher offered him not only a contract for a book on Vietnam, but also one for a book on the . . . Newark project.[18]

Hayden returned to Newark, but devoted much of his time to writing articles and traveling to speaking engagements. By now, he had become a fixed star of the New Left.

Hayden's condemnation of the American government became more bitter. By continuing the war, the government was contravening justice and humanity and therefore losing its legitimacy. Hayden thought that if the American people were educated about the war, they would reject U.S. involvement overwhelmingly. To Hayden, the military-industrial beneficiaries of the war were erecting barriers to prevent this enlightenment; overcoming these barriers became an obsession.

The Newark ghetto riot in the summer of 1967 gave Hayden the final push into the peace movement. Kirkpatrick Sale, in his book on the history of SDS, discussed the difficulties that ERAP workers encountered in the ghettos. Most of the organizers were middle-class college youths whose expectations and values differed from those of the people they were trying to help. They were greeted with suspicion and often with contempt. Sale noted that the poor were unlikely to lead their own campaign for gradual social change when their primary concerns involved obtaining their next meal or rent payment. "ERAP, then, suffered from the incurable disease of having the wrong kind of organizers with the wrong choice of methods operating in the wrong place at the wrong time." [19]

NCUP lasted about two years longer than the other projects largely because of Hayden's leadership. The Newark riot showed that the poor were taking matters into their own hands. "That summer proved to be the death of NCUP, for it was the fourth summer of black rebellion and it (along with the whole growth of black power) finally convinced the young whites that they were unwanted and unneeded in the black ghettos." [20] Having gained prominence in the national antiwar movement, Hayden decided that it was "wise for me to leave, good for me to leave." [21]

From Newark, Hayden planned to move to Chicago to work with the National Mobilization to End the War in Vietnam in organizing demonstrations during the Democratic National Convention in August 1968. However, he was diverted by the student takeover of buildings at Columbia University in April. Feeling that "it would be terrible if the revolution actually started and I was driving across the country," he went to New York and helped to capture and barricade the Mathematics Building at Columbia. [22] The takeover struck him as a prototype for student action across the country. Protest was becoming more violent, and groups everywhere were becoming more extreme in their resistance to authority. SDS was espousing "armed struggle" and revolution, the Black Panthers were at their peak, and Abbie Hoffman and Jerry Rubin had founded the Yippies. The People's Park confrontation in Berkeley occurred the following month. The New Left had become militant, and Hayden moved with it. From Columbia, Hayden continued on to Chicago and his work with the National Mobilization.

After the Chicago demonstrations, Hayden was indicted as one of the Chicago 7, charged with conspiracy and incitement to riot. During the trial in late 1969 and early 1970, he was at the peak of his fame. He coordinated the defense of the seven, a task he later described as "the worst organizational ordeal of my life."[23] In the words of Peter Collier, an editor of the now-defunct radical magazine *Ramparts*, "Indictment as one of the Chicago 7 had authenticated his standing as our leading radical; it was equivalent in our movement to receiving the Congressional Medal of Honor."[24] At the end of the twenty-week trial, Hayden and four others were convicted of contempt of court and of conspiracy with intent to incite a riot.[25] The conspiracy convictions were overturned in November 1973 by a U.S. Court of Appeals due to Judge Julius Hoffman's "deprecatory and often antagonistic attitude toward the defense," the prosecuting attorneys' behavior, which "fell below the standards applicable to a representative of the United States," and other procedural irregularities.[26] In December 1973, a U.S. District Court judge dismissed most of the contempt charges and refused to pass sentence on the rest.

From 1969 to 1971, Hayden lived in Berkeley. During

the Chicago 7 trial, he flew to California on weekends, returning to Chicago on night flights to appear in court on Monday mornings. As an example of the kind of society he envisioned, Hayden formed the Red Family, a commune that gained something of an elite status in Berkeley. The Family pursued collective action (group consensus had to be obtained for the simplest of individual actions, monogamy was discouraged, etc.) and would haggle for hours over "the proper view toward North Korea's [Premier] Kim Il Sung" or whether it "constituted 'privatism' to close the door when using the bathroom."[27]

Fully convinced that the country had to be redeemed through revolution, Hayden became overtly militant. He idolized the Black Panthers, once demanding early payment for a *Ramparts* article so that he could buy gas masks for them.[28] He supported the Weathermen, later calling them "the natural final generation of SDS, the true inheritors of everything that had happened from 1960 on."[29] He founded the International Liberation School, which trained prospective revolutionaries in karate, psychological toughness, and, eventually, the use of firearms (the school held secret rifle practices and kept a stock of ammunition and weapons in the Berkeley hills).[30]

In the Red Family, Hayden was "the star, the theorist-orator, the spokesman for white radicals in America,"[31] but his status conflicted with the commune's strict philosophy of egalitarianism. In 1971, he was denounced by his lover, Anne Weills, for "bourgeois privatism" and "elitism."[32] "It was sick. The resolution of the competitive rivalry between myself and Anne, with everyone else participating in the ritual killing of the father figure. What humiliation and what loss. The jackals of the movement, all those who lived to see idols destroyed, were out spreading the word,"[33] said Hayden. Broken and dispirited, he moved to Los Angeles, living for a time under an assumed name.

To move from SDS to NCUP into the fore of the antiwar movement had constituted a major transition; to be thrown out of the Red Family brought another. He ended his revolutionary militance and crept slowly back into mainstream political action by campaigning for George McGovern in 1972 "not because McGovern is 'different' but because the American government faces a truly desperate situation."[34] His willingness to support a political candidate reflected a severe departure from the Berkeley Hayden who had advocated overthrowing the country by guerrilla warfare. He still believed that the government was corrupt and still concentrated on opposing the Vietnam war, but now he did so by conventional means.

In 1971, Hayden met Jane Fonda at an antiwar rally in Ann Arbor. Fonda was a latecomer to the New Left, but she soon gained prominence due to her tireless support of radical causes and her bitterly resented trip to Hanoi in 1972.[35] Hayden and Fonda organized the Indochina Peace Campaign (IPC) and traveled the country calling for the immediate withdrawal of all U.S. military personnel from Southeast Asia. After the Paris accords ending U.S. involvement had been signed, the IPC still worked to make politicians pledge "to prohibit American reintervention in Indochina . . . to abide by the political provisions of the peace agreement [and] to stop all nonhumanitarian financial aid to [South

Vietnamese President] Thieu and [Cambodian Marshal] Lon Nol."[36]

Hayden and Fonda were married in 1973. From the very beginning, their relationship has been a political as well as an emotional partnership. When asked what had first attracted him to Fonda, Hayden replied, "It was a mutual recognition of the importance of Vietnam." Political considerations even prompted them to get married after Fonda had become pregnant. "We said, 'Well, we're going to have this kid. If we're not married, it'll cause all kinds of unreasonable criticism and divert attention from what we're trying to say. So maybe we better get married.'"[37] Romance brought together an ideal political alliance. Fonda has benefited from Hayden's political skill, and he has gained from her fame and wealth.

Hayden completed his transition to conventional politics by running for the U.S. Senate from California in 1976. By campaigning hard and enlisting celebrity support from Hollywood, he took a surprisingly large share of the vote (almost 40 percent) in the Democratic primary against incumbent John Tunney. Some attribute Tunney's loss in the general election partially to Hayden's primary challenge.

Out of his campaign organization, Hayden formed the Campaign for Economic Democracy (CED), which has been his vehicle in California ever since. The campaign's platform embraces a wide range of liberal-left causes, most notably the abolition of nuclear power and the development of "soft" energy sources such as solar and wind power. CED also advocates a more fundamental change in the country's political and economic system—the establishment of Economic Democracy. This would entail the "democratization" of large corporations by placing community, consumer, and employee representatives on corporate boards of directors.

Since 1976, Hayden has succeeded in forging an alliance between CED and Jerry Brown. In 1972, Brown (then California secretary of state) had helped to prevent the California legislature from passing a resolution branding Fonda a traitor because of her trip to Hanoi. Partly as a result, Brown "had new allies on his side" when he ran for governor in 1974.[38] CED also supported Brown for president in 1980 (members did much of the work in Brown's campaign during the Wisconsin primary). Fonda reportedly used her contacts in the entertainment business to raise as much as three million dollars for Brown's 1980 campaign.[39]

Apparently, Brown sees the connection with CED as a way to broaden his appeal. According to one Brown contributor, the governor responded to angry supporters questioning his alliance with the CED by pointing to Tunney's fate: "Look, do you see John Tunney in the United States Senate? No. Want to know why? Because—he didn't protect his left flank; he let Hayden get to him. I'm not that dumb. So . . . I throw a few bones to Tom and Jane."[40] His tie with CED allows Brown to maintain a link with the liberal-left wing of the Democratic party.

For Hayden, the alliance offers legitimacy and access to influential positions. Brown has appointed him to the Southwest Region Border Commission, a group of representatives from Texas, New Mexico, Arizona, and California that works with Mexico on border policy, and to the board of Western SUN (Solar Utilization Network), a planning and development agency that allocates funds for solar energy in the western United States. Governor Brown also accompanied Fonda and Hayden on part of their fifty-city prosolar/antinuclear tour in late 1979.

Hayden continues to make alliances with prominent political figures and organizations. He recently spearheaded the formation of a coalition of organizations to investigate toxic waste. Members of the coalition include the California AFL-CIO, Friends of the Earth, the Sierra Club, the League of Women Voters, and of course, CED. U.S. Representative Ron Dellums (from Oakland, California) is a CED member, as is former California Lieutenant Governor Mervyn Dymally. Hayden has courted the support of United Farm Workers President Cesar Chavez, Ralph Nader, and United Auto Workers President Douglas Fraser. In 1978, Hayden presented Jimmy Carter with a copy of *Working Papers on Economic Democracy*, a lengthy report by the California Public Policy Center, a CED affiliate. In his own account of the meeting, Hayden said, "I was not exactly Martin Luther nailing an Economic Bill of Rights to the White House door, but at least our ideas had reached [Carter's] desk."[41] With his radical past shadowing him, Hayden uses his new political ties to show that he has become respectable and responsible as well as to gain publicity and influence.[42]

Hayden fully expects his power to grow. His 1976 campaign slogan—"The radicalism of the sixties is the common sense of the seventies"—reflects his belief that many of the ideas developed by the New Left are becoming acceptable to most Americans. Whether or not it is true that a radicalism that once was isolated and alien to American society will become a force at the center of society, the radicalism of the 1960s is the foundation on which Hayden is building CED and his career.

> It's coming; we're going to take over. The last few administrations have all been controlled by the generation of World War II. The next big generation will be those who came to political life during Vietnam. My generation. The country will be under our influence for a long time to come.[43]

Hayden has always believed that the society he foresees will eventually be established. An important difference between his thinking now and in the 1960s is that he has learned to be patient. He awaits the time when "those who filled the streets in the 60's may yet fill the halls of government in the 80's."[44]

There is little doubt that Hayden is a formidable figure. Democratic National Committee member Mary Warren has said, "Whether you like Hayden or not, you have to recognize his strengths. He's intelligent, he's his own man, and he's an excellent organizer. You can't sell him short."[45] With CED behind him, he is not to be taken lightly. Gray Davis, a former aide to Governor Brown, explained, "It's as simple as this: He has the troops, and he has the funds. You ignore him at your own peril."[46]

the
designs of
violence

2

the nation's problems, in Hayden's mind, result from the unconstrained power of both the federal government and large corporations. Throughout his career, he has called for the establishment of a more "legitimate" system that would give Americans more direct control over the country's political and economic policies.

> I consistently have believed in a participatory democracy, the idea that citizens ought to have a say in the decisions that affect their lives. I felt that way about civil rights in the South; I felt that way about the Vietnam war, which was conducted without our consent; I feel that way about the way the federal government and the oil corporations are carrying out energy policy today. I have always felt that if

> citizens had more of a say we would have a more
> sensible society.[1]

Hayden has consistently raged against manipulative control and has promised a more equitable distribution of power. Although the demand for more equality is compelling, it is important to recognize what sociologist Herbert Gans has described as the inevitable flaw of seeking one value at the expense of others. "The major defect of complete equality is the defect of all single-value conceptions: if equality is the all-encompassing goal, then all other goals, regardless of their desirability or necessity, become lower in priority, and no society can function by pursuing one goal above all others."[2] In the early 1960s, Hayden's conviction that ordinary Americans had "little active control" over their lives grew more intense.[3] He saw how hard it was for the disadvantaged to acquire power and attributed their unfavorable situation to the position and status of the privileged classes, which were constantly trying to maintain their own power. Whites in the South used violence to deny basic constitutional rights to blacks, and, to Hayden's chagrin, the federal government was reluctant to intervene. To Hayden, such injustices revealed an open contempt for the egalitarian ideals on which the country was founded.

The Port Huron Statement pointed to inconsistencies between what the government said and what it did.

> The declaration that "all men are created equal . . ."
> rang hollow before the facts of Negro life in the
> South and the big cities in the North. The pro-

> claimed peaceful intentions of the United States
> contradicted its economic and military investments
> in the Cold War . . . We witnessed, and continue to
> witness, other paradoxes.[4]

SDS was not merely an organization supporting a few isolated liberal policies. It was a vanguard in the crusade for the redemption of pure American ideals. As Hayden put it, "These trends were testing the tenacity of our own commitment to democracy and freedom and our abilities to visualize their application to a world of upheaval."[5] Eliminating poverty, racism, and international tension was a moral imperative.

During the early 1960s, the left still hoped that the nation's problems could be addressed through peaceful political and economic reform. In 1961, Hayden rejected the possibility that radicals in America would use violence. "Probably the effectiveness of nonviolent techniques, the stability of American politics, and the high value students place on human life would, in any case, prevent students from turning to more destructive methods."[6] Hayden's work in Newark was an attempt not to overthrow the municipal government but to ensure the poor their rightful place within it. NCUP tried to teach the poor that they could claim their power as citizens by recognizing their dignity as human beings. "We are trying to organize around the feeling of being poor and powerless . . . We are also trying to organize so that poor people develop a consciousness of themselves as worthwhile human beings."[7] If the poor could be aroused in spirit, they would become strong and flourishing.

After the Hanoi trip, Hayden aimed his moral strictures against the war. In *The Other Side*, he and coauthor Staughton Lynd excoriated the war's immorality:

> Bearing in mind the Nuremberg definition of "wanton destruction of cities, towns or villages" as "war crimes" and "inhumane acts committed against any civilian population" as "crimes against humanity," you read . . . of the bombing of a village in South Vietnam by United States planes which . . . struck without warning at a time when no one was in the village but women, children and old people.[8]

To Hayden, anyone who did not advocate the immediate withdrawal of U.S. forces from Vietnam was immoral, and anyone who missed any opportunity to resist the war was at the least morally deficient, if not thoroughly evil.

At first, Hayden believed that the war would end quickly once its horror was brought to the attention of the American people. Continued involvement in Vietnam convinced him that the government had no interest in responding to the will of the people.

> The crisis lies in the fact that foreign-policy decisions as a whole including those about Vietnam are made essentially without the democratic participation of the American people in a system which was really never set up to democratically involve people in foreign policy.[9]

The war was not just a mistake, but a symptom of widespread corruption. Vietnam provided "an international dimension to the violence and racism we were already seeing at home." By continuing the war, the federal government showed complete disregard for the American people. Nor was Washington unique. Municipal agencies in Newark were "more oppressive than . . . representative institutions for the people in the ghetto." [10] The war deepened Hayden's conviction that the government, by not responding to the needs of the people, was not legitimate.

> An elementary lesson began to dawn on us, a lesson that never was taught us in our civics classes, and that lesson was simply that law serves power. Law serves power. So, despite the literal meaning of the Declaration of Independence and the Constitution, the South would remain segregated. [11]

The nation was so corrupt that all reform efforts would be suppressed.

> . . . now the question is whether or not the original worst fears and worst predictions of the people called the New Left will turn out to be so true that there won't be any operating room for any Left, New or Old. [12]

Hayden's experiences in the South, in the ghetto, and in Vietnam contributed to his loss of faith in the chances for conventional methods of reform.

> Having tried available channels and discovered them meaningless, having recognized that the es-

tablishment does not listen to public opinion—it
does not care to listen to the New Left—the New
Left was moving toward confrontation.[13]

"The People," he said, were truly represented by revolutionaries both in the streets of America and in the jungles of
Vietnam. The Panthers, like the Viet Cong, he wrote in his
account of the Chicago trial, "rely on popular support, not
on coercion, for their success."[14] His strategy for dealing with
government oppression aimed against "popular" groups
such as the Panthers was similar, if more militant, to that for
combating poverty in Newark—the establishment of local
groups struggling for power.[15] Revolutions are made, he
taught, "when the small groups . . . form and fight to control their neighborhoods and their institutions." The Viet
Cong was an example of an organization of "neighborhood
revolutionary committees."[16] Hayden's plan was to form
"liberated zones" that would serve as bases from which
guerrilla bands could emerge to disrupt unliberated parts of
the country.[17]

Hayden's extremist pronouncements were buttressed
by his unrelenting emphasis on the morality of advocating
dissent. Further, the New Left's desire for greater democracy had considerable emotional appeal. To Hayden, whose
hopes for governmental reform had withered, revolutionary
change was virtually a moral necessity. The final stimulus to
militancy seems to have been the 1967 Newark riot. Impressed that the riot was "more effective against gouging
merchants than organized protest had ever been," Hayden
foresaw other possibilities:

> The role of organized violence is now being care-
> fully considered. During the riot, for instance, a
> conscious guerrilla can participate in pulling police
> away from the path of people engaging in attack-
> ing stores. He can create disorder in new areas the
> police think are secure. He can carry the torch, if
> not to all the people, to white neighborhoods and
> downtown business districts. If necessary, he can
> successfully shoot to kill . . . These tactics will be
> defined by the authorities as criminal anarchy. But
> it may be that disruption will create meaningful
> change.[18]

Hayden later claimed that these statements were only de-
scriptions, not endorsements, of how others could use violence. However, to many who have followed Hayden's career, this explanation is no more persuasive than some of his
other current denials.

In the *New Republic*, political writer Richard Parker reported that as a group of former New Leftists watched Hayden on television, Hayden's announcement that he had never
supported violence in the 1960s, had never been a revolutionary, and had never been a Marxist "surprised all who
knew him at the time on all counts."[19] There is much to
corroborate Parker's impression. In *Power on the Left*, a
chronicle of U.S. radical movements, journalist and author
Lawrence Lader reported that Hayden had appeared bran-
dishing a carbine at a campaign rally for Paul Jacobs, a Peace
and Freedom party candidate for the Senate in 1968.[20] On
student violence, Hayden wrote:

> In the future it is conceivable that students will threaten destruction of buildings as a last deterrent to police attacks. Many of the tactics learned can also be applied in smaller hit-and-run operations between strikes: raids on the offices of professors doing weapons research could win substantial support among students.[21]

He accompanied such rhetoric with active support of the Black Panthers, the Weather Underground, and his own International Liberation School, which had been established to train revolutionaries.

In 1969, he coauthored an article that exhorted confrontation rather than passive dissent on the premise that "our goal should always be to apply as much force as possible in an attempt to destroy the social order."[22] Hayden denounced peaceful demonstration as ineffective and counterproductive because it diverted energies from the all-important revolution. Peter Collier, a contributing editor of *California Magazine*, recalled one particularly revealing incident from Hayden's days in Berkeley:

> One day Hayden came to my friend David Horowitz's back yard and announced that he felt it was time to form a new "communist party" replete with an underground, democratic centralism, the works. Horowitz complained that history showed that a party based on that kind of vanguardism would inevitably become totalitarian. Hayden dismissed such quibbles as "anti-Stalinist bullshit." It was

a time when Stalin was undergoing rehabilitation among certain circles in Berkeley.[23]

Now that Hayden is trying to cultivate an image of a respectable politician, it is not surprising that he wants to play down and, if possible, avoid discussion of his days as a militant radical. "I don't like to dwell on it," he has said. "I don't want to rehash 1968."[24]

In the late 1960s, one of Hayden's ploys was to portray the establishment as itself a user of violence in achieving its ends. In a speech at UCLA soon after the Chicago demonstrations, he listed examples of violence in American history, including the War of Independence, "the murder of the Mexicans and Indians," industrial growth ("Mark Hopkins could have taught Joseph Stalin a thing or two about forced industrialization"), slavery, labor struggles, and, of course, Vietnam.[25] Since violence was a revered institution in America, he reasoned, the government's denunciation of New Left violence was just a facade aimed at discrediting the politics of the New Left.

To Hayden, such suppression was oppressive and undemocratic. Claiming that "our violence is not yet equivalent to the three minute violence of a B-52 raid on South Vietnam,"[26] he thought revolutionary violence justified by the violence of the American government.

> I believe that violence should never be ruled out as a method of change, especially, I believe that a country that is burning up Vietnam has no right to lecture people to be nonviolent.[27]

Furthermore, the government's use of force against the violent tactics of the New Left was clear proof that it lacked authority.

> . . . violence in this country stems from a system which is sick . . . which is therefore losing authority and legitimacy in the eyes of millions of young people in this country . . . a system which relies more and more on the use of force, on the use of police, to maintain itself rather than relying on consent or persuasion or traditional techniques of democracy.[28]

In other words, New Left violence demonstrated that the government lacked any semblance of moral authority and that the government was therefore illegitimate, thereby justifying further New Left violence. Hayden never made clear why revolutionary struggle was legitimate even though the New Left's tactics were not based on "consent or persuasion or traditional techniques of democracy." Apparently, he was so convinced of the moral imperative of revolution that any consideration of democratic means became irrelevant.

Dave Dellinger, another of the Chicago 7 defendants, pointed to the New Left's failure to acknowledge its own double standards by citing one of Hayden's comparisons between the violence of a B-52 strike and that of the New Left:

> Tom's comparison is statistically correct, but you can't be statistical about violence . . . When the American Government intervened in Vietnam, it never imagined that victory would prove so elusive or the toll in human life so staggering. We have no

way of foretelling—or justifying—the toll in human lives that will follow any attempts we (meaning the New Left) might make at military victory.[29]

Although Dellinger agreed with Hayden on the relative violence of Vietnam and the New Left, he understood that
abandoning consistent standards—that is, responding to
wrongs with more wrongs—could make the New Left just
as reprehensible as the government.

Zealots often divide the world into "friends," who
strictly follow the dogma of their movement, and everyone
else—the "enemy." An advocate of a cause seldom recognizes or tolerates shades of disagreement, and moderation
places a person in the enemy category. Accordingly, Hayden
was unable to perceive any redeeming qualities in nonrevo-
lutionaries. Before the House Un-American Activities Committee in 1968, he testified that he was "not nonviolent,"
which prompted South Carolina Representative Albert Watson to ask if this meant that Hayden believed in violence.
"No more than you do," Hayden replied. "Probably less
than you do."[30] Since Hayden saw violence as embedded in
the government, he regarded Watson (as a member of Congress and therefore an agent of the government) as a propo-
nent of violence. In general, he held anyone opposed to the
revolution responsible for society's failures regardless of the
individual's beliefs. It seemed to many that Hayden's self-
serving moralism led him to develop a prejudice as strong as
any he may have encountered in the South.

At the same hearing, Hayden offered a defense of revolution that was often used by left-wing activists in the late

1960s and early 1970s. When Representative John Ashbrook remarked that the taking over of university buildings was illegal, Hayden replied, "I think it is unconstitutional for the Columbia Board of Trustees to be appointed for life." He denied that it was wrong to prevent other students from going to class, saying that it is "illegal and unconstitutional for scientists to make weapons which are banned by the Geneva agreements and other international treaties, and to make them on university campuses."[31] He also maintained that the Chicago demonstrations in 1968 had been aimed at disrupting the Democratic convention because the delegates lacked authority in our illegitimate system. At the same time he condemned the authorities for breaking up the New Left demonstrations. Hayden's moral outlook was uncomplicated: whatever helped the New Left was good; anything or anyone supporting the prevailing order was bad. Militant dissent was justified because it was militant dissent in behalf of the "right" principle. The tactics of confrontation or revolution were good by definition.

The urgency of change apparently led Hayden to jettison practical considerations. In 1966, Hayden called for the complete control of universities by students and faculty. When confronted with the possibility that the tasks of administration might be intolerable when added to the heavy load of academic work, he replied, "Better exhaustion than the present system of nearly total administration control of the universities."[32] During the 1960s, the left criticized universities for doing "immoral" research for the federal government, particularly for the Department of Defense. Referring to the New Left's demands on Columbia University,

Hayden wrote that the Columbia students "want a new and independent university standing against the mainstream of American society, or they want no university at all." [33] The call for the death of an institution if it could not be redeemed is ironically reminiscent of the comment (much derided by the New Left) of a young officer in Vietnam: "We had to destroy the village in order to save it."

Hayden's judgment that society had to be changed quickly to forestall doom was foreshadowed in the final sentence of the Port Huron Statement: "If we appear to seek the unattainable, as it has been said, then let it be known that we do so to avoid the unimaginable." [34] The eminent social philosopher Sidney Hook recalled that a few years later, when Hayden was asked about the goals of the New Left revolution, he replied, "We haven't any! First we'll make the revolution, and then we will find out what for." Fueled by moral outrage, this view dealt only with destruction of the status quo without regard to an alternative. It was, in Professor Hook's words, "the politics of absurdity." [35]

Hayden rejected a major tenet of the civil rights movement often proclaimed by Martin Luther King, Jr.—the principled acceptance of punishment for civil disobedience. As Hayden explained:

> If you decide that someone's authority now must be put into question because of the blind and insane way that he has used his authority, then you don't want to grant him the right to punish you for doing what you consider to be far more legitimate and moral than what he has done. [36]

He argued that the government, lacking legitimacy, did not have the authority to punish New Left lawbreakers. To Hayden, there was no cause more moral than revolution—his revolution. The conventional standards of civil disobedience and dissent were irrelevant.

In the view of many observers, however, the absence of consistent and well-defined standards undercut Hayden's unceasing attacks on the country. Whether America's history had been one of violence, or whether U.S. involvement in Vietnam was immoral, did not seem to most Americans to justify the reckless use of violence by the New Left. In response, Hayden merely argued that the violence of the government was evil and that New Left violence was laudable and responsible. He never felt it was necessary to develop a more consistent set of principles that might have lent more credence to his views.

Although Hayden now downplays his own involvement in New Left militancy, he does not say (and never has said) that violence is wrong. He says only that violence is no longer required to achieve reform. By 1972, he had become less of an open revolutionary, although he still believed that violence might be necessary because those in power would use force to resist change.

> I'm hardly one who believes that peaceful reform towards the kind of changes I'm talking about is going to happen. I think people ought to draw the lesson that our country is run by murderers . . . If some of our officials use violence everywhere else in the world, there's no doubt that they would use it

> here . . . there is no residue of hope within regular
> channels, only violence awaiting you.[37]

Here, Hayden appeared not to be the vocal advocate of violence he once was, but someone almost stoically resigned to
the inevitability of violent confrontation.

Over the next few years, Hayden came to feel that the
public had become more sympathetic to radical goals because of its increasing disapproval of the Vietnam war and
growing support for social reform through government action. "The more militant demonstrations of the '60s," he
said, "woke people up and created a few changes, and laid a
base for being able to work somewhat within the system."[38]
By 1974, Hayden had a reason for saying that violence was
no longer necessary.

> It's not a question of our forcibly overthrowing the
> established order; it's a question of people getting
> organized to work within the system to a point
> where the majority of people are at least sympa-
> thetic to fundamental change. If at that point vio-
> lent repression starts, as it often does, I would
> rather deal with it politically than to resort to
> counterviolence . . . I can't conceive of picking up
> the gun except in extreme cases of self-defense.[39]

In a 1972 interview with *Rolling Stone* magazine, Hayden
discussed the Weather Underground, a faction of SDS that
had broken away in 1968 and was responsible for assorted
acts of arson through 1972. The group was misguided in its
use of violence, he said, because it had misread the mood of

the American people. He offered the example of someone who might stumble into a restaurant saying that he had just been beaten by the police:

> . . . Anyone in America will now, with few excep-
> tions, believe that that would have happened. That
> kind of climate of distrust of the government, dis-
> trust of the police, is there, and if you understand
> that, you understand that the Weatherpeople were
> wrong in believing that the American people were
> impossibly conservative.[40]

Hayden did not condemn the Underground for its violence, but only for its failure to recognize that Americans could be reached by other means. The implication was that if the American public were "impossibly conservative," then violence would have been justified. Hayden abandoned violence not because the American people were against it, but because he now claimed that public opinion had moved closer to his own vision of things and to the politics of the New Left.

Hayden still hopes to say last rites over America's economic system. The success of capitalism, he believes, has been tied to the greedy exploitation of resource frontiers. When the nation was founded, "the rights to vote and own property seemed equally sacred and complementary. The boundless frontier seemed to guarantee a free path to expanded economic and political freedom."[41] As the nation grew from one ocean to the other, the seemingly endless supply of land, raw materials, and expanding markets assured the growth of the capitalist economy.

Hayden continues to charge that violence was an inherent element of American economic development. As part of the need to destroy resistance to the economic juggernaut, Indians were "silenced in the violence of industrialization and acquisition." [42] When American business reached its limits in North America, it went abroad seeking further expansion of resource and market bases. Hayden often has likened the motives behind U.S. involvement in the Third World to those that fueled the conquest of Native Americans.

But the capitalist frontier, Hayden warns, is coming to an end. We are "reaching the end of the petrochemical age" as cheap fossil fuels become unavailable. [43] Nonrenewable resources are nearly depleted, and the loss of the infinite frontier foreshadows doom for America's economic system.

> The 1970s became a fast downhill slide for America's empire and sense of national self-confidence. "The America Century" proclaimed by *Time* in the 1940s had led instead to a world of Khomeinis. Our former competitors, Japan and Germany, were re-emerging from the ashes of World War II to outperform us in the international market place. Our economy developed simultaneous tendencies to recession and inflation. Real disposable income began to sink for the first time in anyone's memory . . . Worst of all, instead of an abundant frontier, it appeared that we were running out of every resource, beginning with oil, that we had depended on for our way of life. [44]

Hayden seeks to help America escape the pernicious frontier mentality because it is leading the country to disaster.

> Inherent in the process of doing business under capitalism is a market tendency to put profits above people, to lure the consumer into the highest price possible while conceding the lowest wage possible to the workers, magnifying the positive qualities of a product while minimizing its problems. It takes an extraordinary person to succeed in business while being honest and charitable.[45]

Attempts to extend the capitalist frontier would require further exploitation and manipulation of the American people, nourish the base desire for material possession and personal power, and drive the United States into moral decay.

> Most of our artists are employed in the creation of mindless commercials, many of our scientists create weaponry, wife beating and violence against women generally is on the rise, pornography is a bigger industry than movies and recording together, racism is still a part of the national fabric, crime is rampant and, not surprisingly, mental illness is epidemic.[46]

Hayden calls for a reorientation of values and the development of the "human spirit." The new era "needs a new morality in the same sense that the Protestant Ethic served the rise of capitalism." The new morality would embrace "inner, rather than outer rewards, modesty rather than status hunger, love rather than domination." Along with this new morality there would be (once again) an extension of democracy because "the 'inner frontier' can only be enriched by an expansion of democracy" that would encourage people to feel they have control over their own lives. Hayden has always asserted the moral superiority of his own positions and programs, by equating them with the attainment of pure ideals. The founding document of CED echoes in part the sentiments of the Port Huron Statement: "We believe that the human spirit can overcome any obstacle to its freedom." [47]

CED
at the
grass roots

3

in his days as a practicing radical and revolutionary, Hayden always believed that ideas were critically important in the battle for people's minds. Now that he has decided to achieve his goals by working within the system, he knows that the joining of ideas to organization can produce a potent political weapon. He also recognizes that this is especially true in California politics. With a long-standing progressive tradition of nonpartisan local elections, citizen initiatives, and referenda, the state's political environment encourages weak political parties. Unlike the situation in New York, Boston, or Chicago, where machine politics have long dominated local government, political power in California has been wielded by special interest groups and their lobbyists or by powerful politicians such as Jesse Unruh when he was speaker of the Assembly. Elections today are not simply conflicts between the two major political parties but contests between candidate organizations loosely affiliated with either the Republicans or the Democrats. It is into this near organizational vacuum that Hayden has brought CED.

In Hayden's view, an effective organization is not only essential to political success but beneficial to its members, who are thus socialized into new roles and commitments. It is something of a paradox that with his New Left background and often expressed hostility to authority and hierarchy, Hayden has become the new "organization man":

> It is organization that wins victories and assures their implementation. It is organization that keeps people anchored to a larger picture of life than their personal ambitions. It is organization that teaches people how to be citizens rather than private souls, and how to work together instead of at one another's throats. Without organization, people will not commit their lives to social change.[1]

Although CED's prime objective is the achievement of Economic Democracy, its intermediate goal is the election of local and state officials committed to the ideals and policies formulated by Hayden and his close advisers. Hayden's strategy is essentially threefold: to recruit a highly motivated core of loyalists who will create a self-contained and self-supporting political organization within a particular community, to operate within the Democratic party and develop candidates for elections, and to build electoral coalitions with groups sympathetic to CED goals. CED claims that it has supported more than fifty candidates who now hold elective offices around California. It has local chapters in 25 cities, a dues-paying membership of around twelve thousand, and about five hundred dedicated and experienced activists.[2]

CED members overwhelmed local Democratic party caucuses in 1980 to take advantage of changes in party rules. They won a third of the seats at the January 1981 California State Democratic Convention and a third of the seats on the Democratic State Central Committee.[3] At the 1981 convention Hayden began working with Senator Alan Cranston in a bid to revise delegate selection processes for Democratic national conventions. He also took the lead in preventing Ku Klux Klan member Bill Metzger, winner of the Democratic primary for the House of Representatives from Riverside, from controlling convention seats customarily given to primary winners. Hayden hopes to play a decisive role in shaping the direction of the party and moving it toward Economic Democracy. "We want to get hundreds and thousands of CED activists into the Democratic Party. Then we'll get the party involved in local elections and at the precinct and assembly district levels," he says. "If we can do that, we'll elect mayors, county supervisors and city councils as part of a coalition with other interest groups. After we do that, we can elect members of the Legislature."[4]

An internal CED memorandum following the 1981 convention noted the organization's success: "Our goal was to elect 1–2 state party officers as well as delegates to the Executive Board of the party. The result of our effort was the election of 5 of 6 CED-endorsed candidates for state party office including CED activist John Means (Southern Treasurer) and CED member Jack Trujillo (Northern Secretary)." The memo concluded with the following assessment:

> Major elements of the community, labor, elected officials, and Democratic Party regulars have returned from the convention with a new respect for CED both as a constructive force in the party and a real power to reckon with . . . How significant that step was can be gleaned from the success of a subsequent $100-a-plate CED fund raiser. Held at Los Angeles' luxurious Beverly Hilton last November, the event attracted 300 people, including many notable Democratic Party regulars. The master of ceremonies was Peter Kelly, a mainstream Democrat and the party's Southern California chairman. In a recently obtained letter to Tom Hayden, written after the January 1981 convention, Kelly had these warm words: "Thanks for your help at the Democratic State Convention. You and the CED delegates were the cornerstone of my campaign. I am counting on your continued involvement as we begin to rebuild the Democratic Party." [5]

Hayden's appeal to the left-liberal groups within the Democratic party can be attributed to CED's ability to elect men and women to local offices and to raise money. Given his success in getting political foot soldiers to walk precincts in support of CED-backed candidates, Hayden's claim of leading a grass-roots organization is credible. On the other

hand, his efforts at raising money from the same grass roots
are less impressive—in fact, negligible. An investigation by
a liberal-left Berkeley newspaper reported Hayden's "highly
questionable use of state and federal funds." Specifically, it
found that CED had—

> Channeled federal dollars from Western SUN (a
> federal solar energy project) into community action
> groups which are affiliated with Hayden's CED. At
> the same time legitimate solar groups that are not
> affiliated with CED are unable to obtain funding
> from Western SUN.
>
> Put CED members on the payroll at Western
> SUN. Positions in the federal program tend to be
> filled not on the basis of knowledge or ability in the
> field of solar power, but on the basis of classic po-
> litical patronage.
>
> Obtained federal funding from the CETA (Com-
> prehensive Employment and Training Act) program
> to pay wages to CED members for doing work for
> CED. The taxpayer-funded work involved little
> more than political organizing for the Hayden
> organization.
>
> Used a Santa Monica crime control program
> called Communitas, which has a quarter million
> dollars in federal grants, to promote rent control
> and other political projects dear to CED's heart,
> but completely unconnected to crime control.[6]

CED's reliance on federal agencies for funds is no less
revealing than its dependence on Jane Fonda for the bulk of
its general moneys. CED, which owns and receives its profits

from Fonda's Workout, an exercise salon for women, also gets money from her movies. During October, November, and December 1980, according to Justin Raimondo, editor of *Libertarian Vanguard*, "Workout revenue going to the CED General Fund totalled $47,660. During the same period, only $2,692 came from memberships and renewals and just $280 from donations." An internal CED report noted that "we are very dependent on the Workout money. Revenue from memberships and more decentralized methods of fundraising are comparatively non-existent." Furthermore, Fonda is able to raise money for CED through her extensive network of contacts in the show business community. "More big money—this going into CED's Education Fund—comes from Fonda's 'Celebrity' fundraisers. A January 1981 statement, for example, shows that CED received $56,000 raised by Fonda among her 'progressive' Hollywood friends and associates."[7]

By its own admission CED is financially strong, which is one reason why it is taken seriously. Equally important, however—and both supporters and enemies agree on this point—is its organizational strength. CED has a tireless cadre of organizers and precinct walkers who are determined to take over dozens of cities in California and reorient them along CED lines. They have already won control of city councils in Chico, Santa Cruz, and Santa Monica. CED suffered a major defeat in April 1981 when its slate of four candidates, running under the banner of Berkeley Citizens' Action, lost to a coalition slate backed by Democrats, Republicans, landlords, realtors, and the police officers' association. CED's publication, the *Economic Democrat*, described the election result as "a crushing blow after the success of 1979 in which progressives gained a working majority on the council." [8]

It came as no surprise when Hayden announced that in 1982 he would seek the Democratic nomination for the 44th Assembly District, which principally includes the city of Santa Monica on Los Angeles's western flank. He and Jane Fonda have a home there (they also own a 120-acre ranch north of Santa Barbara, California, which they bought in 1977), and it is the site of CED headquarters. If the state of California is the organization's political target—Hayden has pointed out that his organization has nothing to say to the rest of the country if it cannot win in California[9]—the city of Santa Monica has been CED's testing ground in its bid to develop a power base.

The issue the CED chose in April 1979 was rent control—and it worked according to plan. CED proved that this kind of single-issue populism (in other cities it has focused on housing or no growth or toxic waste) can be a successful vehicle for electing a handpicked slate of candidates—in the case of Santa Monica, to the rent control board. As far as CED was concerned, this was the pivotal point of real power in a city where 75 to 80 percent of the eighty-six thousand residents live in rented apartments or homes. Very simply, a "renters' revolt" was born, spearheaded by a grass-roots movement called Santa Monicans for Renter Rights (one of several groups with strong ties to CED), which succeeded in passing one of the strictest rent control laws in the nation. (A judge would rule that the law was "confiscatory" because it failed to assure landlords of a "just and reasonable return on their investment.")[10] Using the initiative process, CED had gained its first major electoral victory.

In April 1981, it scored its second when it won control of Santa Monica's city government as CED members or CED-backed candidates won five of the city council's seven seats. The council majority elected Ruth Yannatta Goldway mayor. Goldway is a longtime friend and political ally of Hayden and the wife of his chief economic theorist, Derek Shearer, a fellow of the Institute for Policy Studies and coauthor of *Economic Democracy: The Challenge of the 1980s.* Shearer was appointed to the Planning Commission. As city attorney, the council named Bob Meyers, an activist legal aid and author of the rent control law.

CED's campaign in Santa Monica was organized on a block-by-block, house-by-house basis, with dozens of full-time staffers involved in the nuts-and-bolts politics of turning out voters on election day who had a vested interest in rent control. Hayden knows that mobilizing tenants (especially old people) who are least likely to move is an effective way of building a permanent political constituency that will help him in acquiring and preserving power. He also knows that pocketbook issues will always attract voters who would have nothing to do with any proposal that had a trace of radicalism but who will support anyone who promises to keep their rents down or to make low-cost housing available.

Hayden has understood what his enemies also knew and feared but could do very little about—namely, that rent control is an emotional issue around which an organization like CED can mobilize individuals and families in their day-to-day life. It deals with housing, which consumes a fourth, perhaps a third, of an average family's income and represents the single largest expenditure in the household budget. Moreover, people spend most of their time in their apartment or house, and everything that affects where and how they live, from the rate of inflation to food, energy, and health care costs, touches on the quality of their life. Among housing issues, rent control is the one most likely to generate "class feelings" of hardship and inequality. It has the potential for certain kinds of mass involvement and collective action. Hayden has been able to capitalize on these feelings of resentment and alienation by making the need and demand for rent control comprehensible—at least in the short run—to everyone. Most important, he has been able to use rent control to build an effective coalition of low- and middle-income tenants who have a common interest in lowering their rent.[11] In the long run, Hayden is counting on such coalitions to look beyond single issues such as rent control and back him in working for other political goals that CED has on its agenda—in other words for Economic Democracy.

Derek Shearer has made no bones about his belief that Economic Democracy is a useful "euphemism for democratic socialism,"[12] that socialism has a bad name "and no amount of wishful thinking on the part of the left is going to change that in our lifetime . . . The words Economic Democracy are an adequate and effective replacement."[13] More recently, Shearer made a similar observation about the visibility of socialism as a concept in America. According to *Barron's*, Shearer suggested to participants at a two-day conference in Washington, D.C., entitled "Taking Charge: The Next 10 Years," that activists should avoid the word "socialism." "We have found in the greatest tradition of American advertising," he told the audience, "that the word 'economic democracy' sells. You can take it door to door like Fuller Brushes and the door will not be slammed in your face." [14] He went on to elaborate on CED's strategy to package rent control for "gut" appeal to the voters:

> Political campaigns are not educational vehicles. What you do is play on [the voters'] feelings and sentiments . . . We sent out a postcard of an elderly family, somewhat haggard—they looked a little bit like an Auschwitz picture. Stamped across their chest was the word EVICTED. We found a senior citizen who was dying of cancer who was being evicted. We reprinted the article [about him in the local newspaper]; the headline was 'Before I Die I'm Going to Vote for Ruth Yannatta and Rent Control.' We distributed that on the door of every tenant in the city two days before the election . . . We considered techniques that played on people's feelings and emotions around a very simple idea: that housing is a basic human right, that it comes before the need to profit. [15]

CED's opponents in Santa Monica have regularly charged that rent control is socialism and a subversion of free enterprise. But as Humpty Dumpty explained long ago, people can always make words mean whatever they want them to mean—especially, one may add, in political campaigns where voters are often moved to action more by slogans and jargon than by reason or sound argument. Shearer has candidly admitted that one of CED's goals is to use the "power of the city to control the wealth of the city." [16] Whether they consider themselves radicals, progressives, or socialists, Hayden and the activists of CED are part of a political movement that seeks (among other things) a majority in power in the city government that will choose programs and reform measures that will lead to better ways of distributing wealth and power. As Shearer emphasized again, this time to reporter Ed Bradley on *60 Minutes*, "It's really a matter of control."

"The net result of economic democracy would be a redistribution of the wealth?" Bradley asked.

"I would hope so," Shearer said. "My own personal bias is that America's a profoundly unequal country." [17]

When Hayden and his CED swept every open seat on the rent control board and city council of Santa Monica, they won what the radical magazine *Mother Jones* aptly described as "Left control—not just representation, but indisputable control—of city hall." [18] A coalition of local tenant associations and labor and senior citizens groups, together with CED, had succeeded in turning the voters into a steamroller that produced a lopsided 54–46 percent victory for the city's tenant forces. Hayden was exultant. "For the first time in the United States, an American city . . . is governed by a mayor and a city council that is committed to economic democracy," he told a Sacramento Press Club luncheon. [19] Although Economic Democracy is not easily defined, those who champion its cause believe that the wealth of a city like Santa Monica, and the potential political power of city government when it is in progressive hands, can be used to implement programs that will promote basic economic and social change. Whether the goals are called populist or socialist, advocates of Economic Democracy perceive them as the only alternatives to the continued dominance of the U.S. economy by corporations.

Hayden believes that CED is creating "a new generation of political leadership" whose electoral tactics differ from those of California's traditional media-oriented politicians. "Jerry Brown tries to organize around ideas," he once observed. "We try to organize around constituencies and candidates." [20] Furthermore, Hayden's basic strategy amounts to a major departure from that used by liberals and progressives in the past. In a twist of political history, labor officials, consumer advocates, environmentalists, and others who are promoting the "new populism" are focusing many of their efforts not on Congress and the White House but on city councils and state legislatures. For the past half century the Democratic party, distrustful of political decisions made at the state level—liberals consistently fought against "states' rights" because it was seen as a code name for racism and segregation—has flexed its political muscles in Washington. There it regularly pressured "big government" to develop federal programs and take responsibilities for virtually every area of lawmaking and policy setting. Today the growing antipathy to too much federal interference in people's lives has shifted the focus of American politics more and more to local communities and statehouses where many of the critical battles will be fought—and where a smaller amount of political force can produce results.

"If Ronald Reagan wants states' rights, we'll give him states' rights," declared a spokesman for a coalition of consumer and environmental groups that won a major battle for Philadelphia workers exposed to potentially toxic chemicals.[21] What frightens many conservatives is that groups like Hayden's CED will ultimately benefit from President Reagan's program of decentralization because their whole method of operation is directly geared to gaining power in local communities, city governments, and state legislatures. Liberals, progressives, socialists—virtually all those who make up the contemporary political left today—are fully aware of the public's disenchantment with the single-minded pursuit of liberalism's "great community" (the Great Society) drawn and bound together by a powerful, progressive central government and by a powerful, progressive president managing the nation's economy and seeking to bring about a more equitable distribution of wealth. No longer are local communities and state governments viewed (in the words of Arthur Schlesinger, Jr.) as "the last refuge of reaction."[22] Hayden and other left-liberal grass-roots activists hope that when President Reagan talks about the decentralization of federal authority, he will decide in favor of local rights over federal regulations, especially when what "the locals" want—local organizations such as CED, for example—is in direct opposition to what Reagan wants nationally. Hayden has never made a secret of his intentions to disrupt as often as he can the Reagan administration's national priorities. Now he sees his chance to command the political and moral high ground that comes with defending civic virtue and public-spiritedness in cities like Santa Monica and with promoting the principles of community and equality as part of the promise of Economic Democracy.

"The New Federalism of the president is really going to open up a tremendous kind of political conflict and battleground," Shearer told Ed Bradley on *60 Minutes*, "and I hope that the end result is a kind of economic democracy solution."

"Today Santa Monica, tomorrow the rest of the country, the world?" asked Bradley.

"Well, we certainly hope so," said Shearer.[23]

the
shape of
economic
democracy

4

not surprisingly, Hayden believes that those who resist his reforms are subverting the will of the people. Now, however, the charge of illegitimacy has shifted from the government to the nation's giant corporations. These, he insists, should be considered public rather than private enterprises.[1] Decisions made by corporate executives with regard to marketing, elimination of waste, and plant operation, for example, affect millions of people every day and largely shape the quality of life. The public, says Hayden (echoing the sentiments of Ralph Nader), has a right to participate in the making of those decisions.

Presently, executives and corporate board members are not sufficiently accountable to the public. "The largest corporations are beyond the traditional market forces, they are beyond the mechanisms of supply and demand, they are be-

yond the traditional concept of regulation . . . there's really
a problem here of unaccountable power."[2] The very nature
of corporate capitalism is corrupt. "We're not saying that
corporate executives are more selfish, venal, criminal or corrupt than anyone [else]. They just have more opportunity to
be selfish, venal and corrupt because they handle more
money and they make more decisions in our name."[3] When
a corporation reaches a certain size, Hayden contends, it
should be considered a public enterprise, and it follows that
the public should have a direct say in its operation.

The institutions traditionally thought to be constraints
on corporate power are no longer believed to be effective.
First of all, the free market economy does not impede the
most powerful (and therefore the most "public") corporations. Hayden cites numerous statistics indicating interlock-
ing directorates and concentrations of power: "Four or five
firms control more than half the market in sectors ranging
from breakfast cereals to oil." (He is wrong about oil.)[4] He
believes that corporate managers use their power and capital
to inhibit competition. As solar energy companies become
established, Hayden laments, "big oil" companies acquire
them and suppress solar technology in order to protect their
own fossil fuel investments. Consumers have an inadequate
choice of products because large corporations "are not
under the control of supply and demand."[5] The country
is cheated, Hayden contends, because companies prevent
the sale of less profitable but more "socially beneficial"
products.

The second constraint that has failed to check corporate
power, in Hayden's opinion, is stockholder control. Share-

holders hold stock for too short a time or in insufficient quantities to wield influence, and those who might be influential (along the lines Hayden would like them to be) have the same selfish desires as corporate managers. "The shareholders' basic interest is dividends, and if that goal is served by shutting down a plant, polluting a well, or keeping bribery a secret, the shareholder will always go along with management's plan." Management decisions and board elections are virtually uncontested. Hayden compares the voting power of stockholders to that of Soviet citizens: "In both cases management proposes a one-party slate, and the elections are little more than a ritual."[6] (As Nader puts it, "Management so totally dominates the proxy machine that corporate elections have come to resemble the Soviet Union's euphemistic 'communist ballot'—that is, a ballot which lists only one slate of candidates."[7]

Although an ardent labor supporter, Hayden feels that unions no longer effectively constrain corporate power. He points to a decrease in union membership and the flight of companies to the South, where unions are less powerful. Blaming the economic slowdown on management, he says that union leverage is deteriorating because of rising unemployment. Management will have increasingly greater strength to refuse unions demands as the economy worsens.[8]

Finally, Hayden complains about the ever-increasing connections between big government and big business. Corporate contributions to election campaigns give companies undue influence in determining who is elected and how officials weigh the interests of business and the public. Regulatory agencies are ineffective because of the close ties that regulators have to the companies they are charged with overseeing: ". . . 350 officials of agencies have roots in the industry they are charged with regulating in the public interest. One hundred officials of drug companies, for instance, are deciding what drugs to sell and what chemicals to put in food."[9] The assumption is that regulatory officials ignore harmful business practices because of previous indoctrination in profit-seeking behavior or because they hope to obtain good jobs in private industry in the future. With big business increasingly involved in electoral politics and regulatory agencies dominated by people with corporate affiliations, Hayden concludes that the government does not and cannot adequately protect the interest of the public against the overwhelming power of this industrial gigantism.

Regulatory agencies, however, are not the only external legal restraints on corporate power. In *Corporate Performance*, business consultant Francis W. Steckmest notes several other distinct types, including (1) state chartering laws and Securities and Exchange Commission (SEC) requirements, (2) competition imposed by the market system, (3) constraining influences of tax laws, (4) direct government controls that regulate corporate performance, (5) public pressure from individuals, the media, and public-interest groups, (6) peer pressure from other corporate managements and business organizations, such as the Business Round Table, that monitor professional reputations and status, and (7) "internal constraint"—voluntary corporate accountability.[10] The environment in which corporations operate has changed in the direction of greater social accountability. In this case, the whole is greater than the parts. Hayden's argument that individual restraints are ineffective ignores the cumulative effect of the various restraints.

In his condemnation of corporate capitalism, Hayden disregards more than a little evidence that corporate power is tempered by many of the very institutions that he claims have failed. In the marketplace, for example, no company interested in increased profits can ignore the desires of consumers. There is no reason to assume that people continue to buy overpriced goods of low quality. The fact that they do not is clear—witness the financial difficulties of the American automobile industry. It is one of the most concentrated industries in America and contains three of the nation's largest corporations. Chrysler remains in business only because of government-guaranteed loans, partly as a result of its failure to produce automobiles that consumers wanted. While millions of potential customers were becoming attracted to smaller, more fuel-efficient cars, the American auto industry failed to respond quickly enough. It appears clear that size and a concentrated market do not always, or do not by themselves, prove that consumers are powerless in their dealings with a distant and impersonal corporation. Of course, the auto industry is not unique in misjudging its market. Other well-known examples include DuPont's failure with Corfam and Procter & Gamble's ill-fated campaign to persuade the public to prefer Pringles to traditional potato chips.

Labor is well represented in the economy by unions that have emerged in response to past corporate abuses. If companies are fleeing from the industrial Northeast to obtain cheaper nonunion labor in the South, unions will also grow in the South as workers see the need for them. Hayden berates American companies for seeking cheaper labor overseas, but, again, workers will surely respond if they find it in their interests to do so. The *Wall Street Journal* recently reported that the United Auto Workers and other American unions are just beginning to associate with unions from other countries.[11] If world cooperation among workers should ever result, corporations would be less able to hunt for lower wages in foreign nations. Our society is flexible enough that employees will continue to see that they are adequately represented.

The general public—Hayden's "community"—has also supported an array of organizations that serve as a check on corporate power. Environmentalist groups such as Greenpeace and the Sierra Club have flourished in recent years as the American people have become more concerned about environmental policy, and citizens groups have formed in many places to oppose corporate practices. The goals of such organizations are usually met through government regulation. The inability of business to stop legislation proposed by consumer and citizens groups suggests, at the very least, that corporations do not "own" the government. In *Corporate Power and Social Responsibility*, economist Neil Jacoby noted the passage of several laws during the 1960s that business vigorously opposed, including the Fair Packaging and Labeling Act, the Highway Safety and Motor Vehicle Standards Act (both passed in 1966), and the Air Quality Act of 1967.[12] University of California Professor Eugene Bardach has recently concluded that over the "last twelve or thirteen years, business has been forced to accept a vast number of quite costly regulatory impositions in the areas of health and safety practices, environmental protection, hiring and promotion practices, and the disclosure of consumer information. Business interests consistently fought these impositions and almost as consistently lost." [13]

In comparing the present political power of business with that it once enjoyed, Jacoby concluded that "there can be little doubt that the relative political strength of business has fallen dramatically during the past century." [14] Furthermore, there is no monolithic "business interest" for the simple reason that different businesses have different political goals. The steel industry has opposed foreign steel imports; the auto industry has favored them. The increase in political campaign contributions from businesses must be weighed against the increased political activities of unions and other private interest groups that have supported both political candidates and social legislation that business has fought. "The notion that corporate enterprise 'dominates' or unduly influences the American government," Jacoby wrote, "simply does not withstand examination." [15]

Political scientist Ithiel de Sola Pool characterizes the interaction between government and business as a two-way exchange with shifting alliances and no winners and no losers. Moreover, based on research on business activities in regard to foreign-trade legislation, she found that (1) "businessmen's economic interests were rarely clear to them," (2) "businessmen were often extremely maladroit and uncomfortable in the unfamiliar world of the public sector," (3) "politicians mobilized businessmen to serve the politicians' interests as often as businessmen mobilized politicians to serve business interests," and (4) "conflicts of interest within business often serve to preclude action by major business interests, while quite minor business interests might prove effective if not checked by such conflicts." [16]

While Hayden ignores or de-emphasizes the importance of legal and market constraints, his analysis of corporate power is flawed because he equates possession of resources with the possession of power. As James Q. Wilson, professor of government at Harvard, has observed, "One cannot *assume* that the disproportionate possession of certain resources (money, organization, status) leads to the disproportionate exercise of political power. Everything depends on whether a resource can be converted into power, and at what rate and at what price. That, in turn, can only be learned by finding out who wins and who loses." [17]

Thus, Hayden's analysis, appealing as it is to those who want (and find it easy) to distrust large concentrations of power, particularly power perceived to be uncontrolled or unaccountable, suffers from three defects. First, it ignores the historical record that business power has been moderated through a variety of legal constraints. Second, he downplays the importance of market forces and other organizations that interact with corporations. Third, Hayden illegitimately equates control of economic resources with political power. It is only by sidestepping these three flaws that he can propose that Economic Democracy is necessary to curb uncontrolled corporate power.

Despite the variety of checks on American business, Hayden argues that the corporate system is not truly democratic. He proposes putting representatives of consumers, workers, and members of the community on corporate boards to "democratize the boardroom" and thereby constrain corporate power from within. His idea of representation is that everyone affected by the decisions of a group or organization should have the right to participate in the making of those decisions. "The ideal of democracy," he says, is that "consumers and employees and the people who are affected by economic decisions ought to have a bill of rights of participation within the giant enterprise." [18]

But Hayden does not make clear how this test is to be applied as a guide in choosing representatives. By focusing on representation, he has followed what Professor Robert Dahl has called the Principle of Affected Interests. The core of the principle is that "everyone who is affected by the decisions of a government should have the right to participate in that government." The principle lies behind such appealing propositions as "no taxation without representation." But, as Dahl observes, the principle "turns out to be a good deal less compelling than it looks" because difficulties arise in the determination of who is "affected" by a government. [19] This is one of the problems that confronts Hayden's Economic Democracy. In a wholly impractical way, having failed to understand that use of this principle as the sole criterion for the selection of representatives can lead to utter confusion, Hayden offers only a few clues as to how representatives would be selected.

> The "public" representatives might be appointed by government officials or the SEC . . . Consumer representatives might be chosen from the ranks of ma-

jor customers, as defined by their charge accounts or receipts that prove a permanent stake. Or in the case of utilities, consumers could be chosen by changing the regular monthly billing mechanisms periodically into a ballot with information and phone numbers for various "consumer candidates" for the board. Representatives of the community could be elected from the existing political jurisdictions around the plant. Workers could choose their representatives by a process similar to union elections, with the SEC, or perhaps the National Labor Relations Board, certifying the elections.[20]

In his determination to curb corporate power, Hayden has left many of the complex problems of representation unexamined. Without a clearer explanation of Hayden's intended application of the Principle of Affected Interests, it is impossible to imagine how one might conclude that an individual's interest in a corporation was sufficient to justify representation. Who would be considered the customer when a product is distributed through a system of wholesalers and retailers? Would each distributor be entitled to a vote in running the manufacturing firm, or would only those at each level of distribution who bought directly from the firm get a share of control in the company? Would it not be reasonable to include potential as well as current customers of a corporation? For example, most people probably would enjoy frequent travel yet are restricted because they cannot afford airline tickets. Decisions concerning ticket prices affect people who, though they are not customers, might well become customers if tickets were cheaper. To extend the example, potential airline passengers would have an interest in the price of jet fuel insofar as it affected airline ticket prices. Should they be able to vote for the representatives on the boards of fuel companies?

Hayden's plan for Economic Democracy is meant to provide a more equitable distribution of power, yet Hayden gives no hint as to how equal participation in corporate decision making would be achieved. Hayden states that there should be employee and community representatives. But would the few hundred employees of a firm get as much representation as the several thousand members of the surrounding community? In his scheme, consumers would vote for consumer representatives. But would all customers get one vote apiece, or would votes be allotted in proportion to the size of a customer's purchases? If community representatives were chosen from existing political jurisdictions, would homeowners on the edge of a city have as much of a vote as apartment dwellers living next to a plant?

Hayden is silent on these matters. Yet they are not trivial concerns. As a system purporting to be completely fair, Economic Democracy could hardly allow an equal number of votes both to someone who purchased ten dollars worth of a company's products and to someone who purchased a million dollars worth. On the other hand, allotting votes in proportion to the size of purchases might lead to even greater economic collusion than that which exists today. The largest customers of steel manufacturers, for example, are other large corporations. Hayden surely would not give large corporate customers control of the companies from which they buy; yet it appears that not to give them votes according to the size of their purchases would violate the principles of equity that Economic Democracy is meant to advance.

Hayden's vision of Economic Democracy is similarly vague in other respects. During his 1976 Senate campaign, he suggested that no company should hold more than 12 percent of any product market.[21] But beyond expressing an obvious hostility to concentrated power, this suggestion does not contribute much. For example, Hayden does not say how he arrived at the threshold of 12 percent. Nor is there any indication as to how a company's "market share" would be determined. In his book, *In Defense of the Corporation*, business historian Robert Hessen discusses the difficulties one might encounter in trying to define distinct "markets." In response to Ralph Nader's suggestion of a 12 percent market-share limit, Hessen raises the question of how corporations that are diversified would be regarded. General Motors, for example, manufactures electrical appliances, locomotives, and military vehicles as well as automobiles. Furthermore, competition often occurs at the regional or local level so that figures for national markets may be irrelevant. Hessen has described how products themselves defy classification:

> Are mink and fake fur the same industry? Are real diamonds and synthetic diamonds the same? Are a yacht and a rowboat in the same product line? In each case they are, but only if the product is defined in the widest possible usage—furs, jewelry, boats . . . In reality, the competition (i.e., the rivalry for sales and profits) is between mink coats, diamonds,

and yachts even though they are products of three
different industries.[22]

Attempting to define market shares is further complicated
by the competition between substitutes (for example, steel
and aluminum).

Hayden has also suggested that conglomeration should
be outlawed.[23] Yet how would the boundaries between different markets be defined so that companies could recognize
when their businesses become too diverse? By what measure
would newly developed industries be evaluated? Would an
electronics firm be forced to abandon the sale of a new product line just because it represented a diversification of its
output? Limiting markets may seem easy and attractive to
those who hold that large corporations by their nature are
harmful. But is the suggestion of much practical value?

Since all significant decisions in a corporation would
have to be approved by public representatives (or at least
made according to their wishes), management would be hin-
dered in its primary pursuit of producing goods and services. One of management's most important gauges for
achieving consensus on what goods to produce is profits.
Hayden, however, has never been a strong advocate of offering economic incentives to individuals and companies,
claiming that the practice fosters greed. But he downplays
the importance of individual initiative and incentive in a free
and prosperous economy. It is as if he did not believe that
the quest for profit can or should lead to efficiency and
innovation.

Limiting corporate size and market shares even though market manipulation did not exist would stunt economic expansion. Under Hayden's plan of placing a limit on corporations' market shares, relatively inefficient companies would be permitted shares of markets that under the present system go to better managed companies or to those whose workers are more productive. In effect, limiting the size of more efficient and responsibly run companies would result in wasted resources. Currently, competing companies often operate at different levels of efficiency. Efficient companies produce products more cheaply, allowing them to gain a greater share of the market and increase their profits. Eventually, less efficient companies face the choice of overhauling their operations or going out of business. If they improve their efficiency, they can produce more goods with existing resources, which, in turn, increases their own profits and reduces prices for consumers. If they go out of business, the resources they used become available in another part of the economy. In either case, the economy as a whole is strengthened. Hayden seems unconcerned that limiting market shares or corporate size or de-emphasizing profits would destroy much of the incentive involved in this efficiency.

The anticipation of profit provides an incentive for companies to develop new products and take risks to sell them, as the recent development of personal home computers shows. Two companies, Tandy Corporation and Apple Computer, now dominate sales because they took the lead in designing and distributing personal computers. Under Hayden's Economic Democracy, the personal computer market might not have developed. Since no company, under Hayden's suggestion, could possess more than 12 percent of any market, Apple and Tandy would have had to yield most of the market to other companies immediately. Other corporations such as IBM and Hewlett-Packard grew into giants precisely because they took a chance on marketing innovative products in anticipation of market and company growth. The gains that their founders, managers, and investors have received have certainly been justified, among other reasons, because thousands have been given jobs and millions have benefited from the companies' operations.

The problem inherent in the loss of incentives would be felt throughout the economy under Hayden's blueprint for Economic Democracy. If employee representatives on boards of directors resisted layoffs or pay reductions, employees would have less reason to work efficiently once a company reached the maximum allowable size. In short, Hayden appears to have little understanding of the need for growth and drive as spurs to action. He claims that workers want meaning in their work and a rewarding job. But many of them also want material rewards. It is no secret that entrepreneurs and inventors are often motivated as much by the promise of profit as by the satisfaction of producing useful or socially beneficial products.

The importance of profit as an economic incentive is widely accepted in the United States. In *Political Ideology*, Yale Professor Robert Lane wrote that almost all workers he interviewed felt that the very wealthy in America probably deserved their riches because of hard work or education. They accepted the profit-oriented system as one that rewards those who contribute the most to it. Professor Lane also noted that besides the value of equality, Americans are taught such values as the quest for personal excellence. They do not easily shed the conviction that individuals should be rewarded for their talents.[24] British historian J. R. Pole has written of the popular recognition in American history that "a genuinely egalitarian ideology would conflict with the American system of incentive which was just as important to the public conscience and probably more popular."[25] In short, when Americans make choices between competing values, they give high marks to incentive and economic development. Given Hayden's inattention to some of the economic consequences of his plan of Economic Democracy, he would do well to heed Professor Gans's caveat that single-interest ideologies will fail if they ignore other desirable and conflicting interests.

It is evident that Hayden is not concerned with economic prosperity in the traditional sense of the production of material goods. In a 1979 interview in *Barron's*, Hayden was asked about inefficiencies that might arise with implementation of his program. He replied, "Yeah. Inefficiencies will arise in a democracy. What I'm looking for is a process of accountability."[26] Solar energy, he urges, should be used "whatever the possible short-term cost in dollars," and companies should keep their workers, using criteria that protect jobs even in times of weakened profits.[27] Hayden's standard of efficiency is dependent less on economic well-being than on the development of a "humane" or "moral" system in which people would have more control over their lives. His vision of Economic Democracy stems from a belief that legitimacy in the economic system would encourage inner growth and the satisfaction of the human spirit, especially the satisfaction of being free from manipulation. This, in turn, would increase the overall quality of life even if material goods were less abundant. On the surface, his plan appears to give more "power to the people," but a closer look reveals a potential for the growth of a centralized and manipulative political and economic power.

Sacrificing profit and economic efficiency undoubtedly would lead many businesses to ruin. When it became unprofitable to continue operating a plant in a given community, Hayden suggests, closing the plant would be prohibited if it would harm employees or the community. Since unprofitable businesses would have to continue operating, provisions would have to be made to force creditors, for example, to readjust their loans or future sales to the company. Given the disregard for profit and economic efficiency inherent in Economic Democracy, it is not difficult to imagine increased centralized control, with the government (or some such central authority) called on frequently to forestall bankruptcies throughout the country.

Hayden believes that a uniform standard of the "public interest" would have to be followed. If only a few corporations were reformed, those still operating on the old and discredited principles of capitalism would crush the newly directed enterprises.[28] Unless all businesses operated under the same guidelines, one company board might determine that the "public interest" demanded higher wages for employees, whereas another might decide to lower prices to consumers. Some central authority would have to mediate between companies, decide how the "public interest" would be pursued, and then allocate resources in the absence of a free market. Hayden's Economic Democracy, it seems, would involve some sort of new (though not clearly defined) relationship between the government and corporations as part of his strategy to increase the power of the public sector.

Hayden claims to be as disenchanted with big government as he is with big business. However, much of his writing indicates that his disenchantment is capable of easy expansion or contraction. He has often called for government control of the economy as the cure for the nation's social ills. As an SDS worker in Newark, Hayden saw the government as the key to overcoming injustice. It might be overly dominated and influenced by big business and the affluent, but nonetheless it could be redirected to serve justice. Initially, he believed that the government was only using poor judgment in the Vietnam war and that it could be made to see the error of its ways. He had considerable faith in government and turned to more revolutionary solutions only when the problems of Vietnam, poverty, and discrimination were not solved quickly. Even as a militant, he did not repudiate the notion of government control, but only disagreed with current policies. After discovering that revolution was impossible, Hayden renewed his attempt to change the government's decisions and direction and, ever since, has opposed American capitalism (except for small businesses). In 1974, he saw a "need for an economic system where private property is no longer legalized or tolerated, at least with respect to the massive and vital industries." Belief in the irresponsibility of corporate power had convinced him that "true democracy is incompatible with capitalism." [29]

Appearing on *Meet the Press* in 1979, Hayden said, "Socialism . . . means that the government bureaucracy would take over the corporate bureaucracy, and I think that that is a marriage of twin evils." But later in the same program, when asked to reconcile CED's support for a "national planned economy, national health insurance, national welfare reform, stricter federal standards" with his call for a balanced federal budget and a trimming of government bureaucracy, he could only reply, "We wrestle with that problem all the time."[30]

It appears that Hayden's objections to government control stem from disillusionment with previous liberal programs. When he attacks New Deal or Great Society programs, he does so only because they did not go far enough and therefore were ineffective. He objects to government programs not because they are faulty in principle, but because they cannot work under the present economic system. The clear implication is that for government control to be effective, it must be accompanied by a more fundamental revision of corporate capitalism.

In *The American Future*, Hayden gave additional clues to his current view about the role of government in the economy. Along with attacks on corporate capitalism and New Deal liberalism, Hayden criticizes socialism—but without addressing the issue of whether socialism is a viable economic arrangement. Most of the discussion is a refutation of socialist class theory, with the rest simply pointing out that it is a bad idea to build socialism by taking over companies that have failed. "This by no means rules out public ownership or public enterprise as a legitimate alternative, and one which may make a major improvement in people's lives in comparison with the corporate sector," he writes. Indeed, he often suggests that government should control industry, particularly the energy industry. "Public control in the public interest," he promises, "would be the key theme of any transformation of the energy industry," warning that failure to implement public control would "guarantee a future dependency on shrinking resources with all the dangers of inflation, unemployment, pollution, monopoly and war."[31] His ultimate goal is to "create an energy company that is an American energy company, the only kind of energy company we can trust, and use [it] to develop the resources in the public domain."[32]

It is important to remember that today's left-populist movement is committed to controlling the institutions of government (local, state, and federal). Once they are in the right (meaning progressive) hands, they can help provide the radical reforms necessary to restructure the American economy. Unlike orthodox Marxists, who have always favored a doctrine of internationalism, Hayden's anticorporate crusaders want to "liberate the government from the oil companies" and have laced their populist rhetoric with protectionism, nationalism, and hostility to foreign competition. In 1979, Hayden told an audience in Ann Arbor that "we should not allow the private oil companies to buy from Saudi Arabia or from OPEC." What he really appears to want to do—or so it sometimes seems—is nationalize our basic industries. As Justin Raimondo, editor of the *Libertarian Vanguard*, points out, Hayden is aware of the problems with this remedy for "nationalist concerns" and tried to "squirm out of them" before his Ann Arbor audience:

> What holds us back probably is that we're as scared of government bureaucracy as we are of corporate bureaucracy: we're afraid that if we nationalize the oil industry, James Schlesinger will come back from retirement and be made the head of Exxon. We have to be able to liberate government from the hands of the oil industry, and when we're sure we have a government we can trust, then and only then will we be able to take over the oil industry. But that's what we have to move towards. If oil and energy are as crucial to our national security as all of us realize, it's absolutely insane to allow the key to our security to depend on the private profit of big oil. They have to be regulated. They have to be brought under the control of an elected government.[33]

There are many on the left who believe that Hayden objects not to bureaucracy per se but to the fact that neither the business nor government bureaucracy is in his hands—at least not yet. Raimondo gives his own twist to what he thinks Hayden is up to: "Would it really be necessary for Mr. Schlesinger to come out of retirement? Wouldn't another Schlesinger—a Schlesinger 'we could trust'—rise to take his place? Far from 'liberating the government from the oil companies,' the interests of the government and the oil companies would meet and merge; indeed, the oil companies would *become* the government. "This, then," says Raimondo, "is the meaning and end result of Hayden's business/government 'partnership'—an all-around expansion of government power. This is where the interests of the Rockefeller Brothers and the left populists converge: both seek to operate within—and preserve—the corporate state system." [34]

Given Hayden's past faith in the power of the state, his current call for public control of industry, and the prospect of further centralization under Economic Democracy, his present attacks on government control should perhaps be viewed warily.

Hayden's plans do not say how centralization of authority would be avoided under Economic Democracy. Instead of formulating their goals separately, consumer, community, employee, and management representatives on the same corporate board presumably would formulate a common corporate policy. Independent institutions would not exist to espouse interests in opposition to the policies of the expanded corporate board. Most regulatory agencies, Hayden presumably expects, would be phased out because there would be regulators within every company. It might be difficult under such an arrangement for workers to know precisely what their representatives were achieving for them. They would see only the final result in working conditions and benefits and would have no idea whether the company might have been pressed for more. The scope of the problem is widened when public or community representatives are considered. Some consumers might wish to tolerate some safety risk in a product if they were able to buy it more cheaply. Some members of a community might be willing to accept some degree of pollution if it meant increased employment. If representatives on a corporate board formed company policy together, consumers and community members might never be approached for their opinions on such controversial issues as product safety or pollution.

If the government were to enforce Hayden's program as the standard guide for the "public interest," the public might in fact be far less able to express its will than it is today. For example, in choosing between the advantages of small and big business, Hayden expresses the "public interest" as follows: "Most would agree . . . that communities in general are better serviced and healthier for all where there are networks of locally-owned businesses rather than remotely-controlled chains." Hayden deplores the fact that "the small business sector has become a victim of the upheavals and recessions of the 1970s."[35] The picture he paints is of the local corner store struggling to serve the community against the competition of an outlet of some big corporation. An emotional chord of nostalgia is struck. Since Hayden considers the friendly home-owned store more "democratic" than the impersonal chain outlet, one wonders if government under Economic Democracy might decree that all chains should be turned over to local control.

Hayden fails to see that if "most would agree" that local stores are more desirable, they would not be "victims of upheavals and recessions." The truth, of course, is that large chains offer many advantages that local stores cannot match. Many people, of course, prefer to shop in locally owned enterprises where they know the proprietor or enjoy the personal service. Others prefer to buy from chain stores where they often find lower prices and a wider selection of products. Furthermore, the chains may be more stable than locally owned stores because a few chain outlets may be supporting one that is new or one that perhaps is located in a temporarily depressed area where a local store might not be able to survive. This is not oppression by the larger company; it is the offering of a service to local patrons who might otherwise have no store at all. As this example shows, company size alone does not determine good or evil.

If the government categorically discriminated against large businesses, what would happen to consumers who choose to buy from a chain outlet? Are they to be deprived of the goods and services they prefer because Hayden thinks that local stores would be more "democratic"? Because authority would have to be centralized under Economic Democracy, some people would have no choice but to accept the decision that what they used to prefer is not really in their best interest. Even assuming that the authorities in Hayden's scheme would recognize some people's desire for large businesses, the system would still be flawed. Hayden himself has stated the problem inherent in such control by a central authority: "Planning from the top down . . . simply will fail without the involved consent of labor and the public." [36]

Another issue raised by Hayden concerns the use of pension funds. Currently worth some $800 billion, private and public pension funds own a fifth of the country's corporate stock and in 1981 produced about a fourth of all new capital generated throughout the economy. They are invested in order to get maximum returns with minimum risks, which, of course, is what contributors to pension funds clearly want. Hayden, however, apparently thinks this is somehow wrong. He says that pension funds are subject to "irresponsible investment decisions" and suggests the creation of "state banks as custodians" for all this money. "If recovery from recession, without massive tax increases, is going to be possible, it certainly will require a greater control of pension funds in the public interest." Once again, Hayden is prepared to define, in terms of his own political priorities, the meaning of the "public interest." He seems surprised to learn that pension money sometimes is "invested in corporations engaged in anti-union activity." Funds should be "invested in America's future, instead of wherever the rate of return is currently best." [37] But working people have contributed to these funds and expect them to provide the best financial return possible. Although most of them may not always be in a position to decide how their pensions are invested, they would surely be unhappy if they were to learn that the pension fund managers were subsidizing what some individual or group claimed were socially desirable goals but which yielded less than the highest return. Public pension funds today are exploring a variety of investment options, from channeling money into local economies through buying mortgages to assisting struggling young businesses. While those who manage these funds may be prepared to move into more daring ventures, they also have enough skill and good judgment to avoid mixing politics with investment interests and strategies. [38]

Hayden's arguments for the soundness of Economic Democracy rest on his conviction that what he proposes is right for the American people. In 1966, Hayden himself wrote of the dangers to society when decisions are made by a centralized authority: "A managed society is a paralyzed one, in which humane promises go unrealized, dreams die, people stop hoping for anything beyond the necessary evil."[39] The question is whether Hayden has shown how Economic Democracy would avoid fostering a "managed society." Hasn't he offered an alternative that is too simplistic and inadequately developed to be considered practical and one that does not address the problems of economic stagnation and centralized power that his plan portends? "CED is against big corporations. But CED does not have an answer to how you control them and what is the mix of public and private control."[40] As in the 1960s, when he wanted to "make the revolution and then . . . find out what for," Hayden relies too much on denouncing current conditions rather than on presenting a fully reasoned, practical alternative.

Furthermore, his reasoning and arguments today are sometimes as tinged with inconsistency as they were in the 1960s. In 1978, he claimed that passage of Proposition 13, the voter initiative to cut property taxes in California, indicated "a deepening of populist skepticism towards all institutions."[41] He used this argument in defense of the notion that there was grass-roots support for a fundamental change in the nation. More recently, he denounced the proposition as a tool by which rich capitalists were profiting at the expense of the poor.[42] In other words, Proposition 13 showed both that the rich were working to maintain their power and that the people were moving to curb that power. In his evaluation of the international economy, Hayden has stressed that the United States must end its imperialistic exploitation of the Third World and adopt a "global view" that would move the world from "Cold War to interdependence." [43] This seems to indicate that the United States should abandon isolationism and seek to strengthen its ties with other nations. On the other hand, he believes that large corporations actually have harmed America by entering the global economy for their own selfish aims. [44]

Hayden has criticized foreign investment by American companies on the grounds that it takes job and capital away from our country, where they are needed to strengthen the economy. But he warns against the influx of foreign investment into the United States by saying that the economy is being "sold out from under the feet of the American people." He wants investment capital to stay in the country, but he does not want it to come in. He deplores the suppression of economic competition by corporations, yet he wonders "why America's military strength defends Western Europe against Soviet tanks and missiles while permitting a deadly invasion of German and Japanese cars and television sets here at home." [45]

There are other seeming inconsistencies. "Government bureaucracy *is* an obscene burden" (Hayden's emphasis), and government programs will not lead the country to prosperity, he declares. Yet "in our quest for full employment, we can't be sidetracked by those who say that federal spending is not the solution." [46] During his Senate campaign, Hayden supported Senator Edward Kennedy's national health insurance plan. More recently, however, he expressed reservations, fearing that it would only be "another government subsidy to the American medical/insurance empire." [47] Hayden wrote that restriction of the money supply (a policy recommended by, among others, Jimmy Carter and Federal Reserve Board Chairman Paul Volcker) was disastrous because it limited economic growth, but that expansion and inflation really benefit only the big corporations. [48] (Recall that Hayden also says that economic stagnation benefits corporations because it makes them more powerful relative to labor unions.) In an interview with *San Diego Magazine*, Hayden denied the contention that Jerry Brown's failure in the 1980 presidential primaries showed the public's dislike for Brown's program, claiming that "politics is not an easy way for the public to render judgment on issues . . . [or] an avenue for resolving where the public stands on issues." Later in the same interview, he asserted that CED had proved its compatibility with the public's desires because "the test of our effectiveness is whether we win elections." [49] On *Meet the Press*, he said, "We win elections in California that represent the needs of working people and consumers and that is a pretty good test of whether you have popular support." [50] It appears that Hayden applauds the political judgment of the voters only when they agree with him.

Many of Hayden's arguments are unclear or incomplete. For example, he says that "30 percent of American homes (25 million) are without insulation." [51] But if one assumes that some of those homes are in areas with moderate climates, do all of them need insulation? This inconvenient consideration seems to be dropped in the interest of proving the inadequacy of the country's energy policies. Solar energy, he writes, "lends itself to the search for inner frontiers within outer limits, self-determination and personal self-reliance, respect and stewardship towards the environment, solutions woven into the fabric of life instead of imposed from above and afar." [52] This sentiment may evoke a certain humanist flair, but Hayden never explains precisely how solar energy will lead society to these good ends.

Such fuzziness can be found in many parts of Hayden's most recent book, *The American Future*. In attempting to show the irresponsibility of oil companies in failing to provide jobs, he writes that "though oil companies are five of the six largest corporations in California, the oil industry employs only 1.4% of the workers outside agriculture." [53] The example seems to support his argument, but on closer inspection it can be seen that Hayden's use of statistics is inexact. Comparing the percentage of total employment attributable to the oil industry to the fact that some companies are very large is like comparing apples and oranges. A proper comparison would include the percentage of employment and the percentage of total statewide business of the oil industry. Further, although Hayden includes assets or sales from outside California in his calculation of corporate size, he does not include the number of people employed outside California in his employment statistic.

In another attempt to show that corporations are becoming increasingly powerful, Hayden provides a graph showing that "corporate aftertax profits" have climbed steadily. But the graph does not include the more significant consideration of real corporate profits adjusted for inflation.[54] A graph showing the growth of real corporate profits would be a better indication of corporate power, but would not serve Hayden's purposes as well.

In the 1960s, the New Left did not meet the same standards of "legitimacy" that Hayden applied to the government. Today, CED does not always meet the standards he uses to evaluate corporations. Hayden deplores large campaign contributions. Yet Jane Fonda contributed $400,000 to his 1976 Senate campaign. Federal law limits individual contributions to $1,000, but John Tunney's complaint against Fonda's donation was dismissed because California state law considers all assets of married couples to be held in common. Hayden disapproves of leaders who hold on to their positions of power; yet he has been CED's only chairman. "If corporations resist disclosure," he has written, "it is because they have something to hide."[55] But CED has never had an open convention, and its books are closed to the public.[56] Hayden decries government boondoggles given to business; yet the *Berkeley Barb* has alleged that CED has placed workers on the payroll of Western SUN and that Hayden has channeled CETA workers into CED projects.[57] In the words of one California legislator who investigated CED: "We've dug up so many suspicious contracts of theirs it's incredible. There's a pattern of CED using government money for shit like seminars on rent control."[58] One would think that Hayden would insist that his own enterprises meet the same scrupulous standards that he demands of corporate America.

In some ways, the fuzziness and inconsistency of Hayden's positions may be to his advantage, especially in political campaigns. Those who are already alienated from the

American economic and political system are usually ready to accept any denunciation of the present state of affairs without making much of an effort to examine and evaluate the evidence. It is much easier for such people to allow their views to be reinforced by Hayden's criticisms than to analyze his contentions. Followers may forgive the oligarchic tendencies within Hayden's CED (some would call it his autocratic control) or the incomplete articulation of his plans by arguing that some unfortunate expedients are necessary to achieve reform. Yet much of the moralism and simplicity in Hayden's prescriptions—perceived as virtues by the discontented—is viewed with great skepticism by others.

One of the major defects of Hayden's analysis of American corporations is his almost exclusive preoccupation with what he perceives to be their unrivaled power and influence. Some of his concerns are not totally without merit, nor are they new. But his drumbeat of criticism is weakened and therefore less persuasive because of an absence of balance in his observations—very simply, by what he fails to take into consideration. For example, he has virtually nothing to say about the important changes in our industrial social order since the end of World War II that have made it possible for millions of Americans to improve their social and economic position in life. The United States has moved from a rural to an urbanized society in which family-owned enterprises have largely been replaced by big corporations. It has been a dramatic development, one that has changed the face of America. The point that needs to be made (and is missing in Hayden's account) is that the "bureaucratization of corporate life" has paralleled the movement in this country to a more open society. Significant increases in upward mobility have enabled many people from lower-class positions to move into occupations and to earn salaries never available to their parents.

The problem with Hayden's deep-seated dislike of corporate capitalism is that it easily encourages the facile but erroneous conclusion that the so-called American class-structure is controlled more tightly than ever and that the ladder of success in the world of big business is increasingly closed to those from socially inferior origins. Yet the evidence, as Professor Seymour Martin Lipset points out, "clearly indicates that elite positions have become much more open over time." Given the additional fact that higher education is also more widely available in the United States today than in any other country, "it is not surprising that the proportion of Americans who move from lowly backgrounds into elite positions is greatest in this country." [59] At the very least, it is evidence of the vitality of America's capitalist society. Hayden, however, apparently believes it is immaterial, perhaps because it falls in the category of what the German sociologist Max Weber called "inconvenient facts." In any event, he does not deal with it. If he did, his enmity toward corporate America might be tempered by some understanding and acknowledgement that people on the lower rungs of the social ladder continue to believe (more so than those in other Western industrialized countries) that ambition and hard work can still pay off—in a word, that the belief in equality of opportunity is still very much alive.

retrospect
and
prospect

5

tom hayden is attempting to bridge the gulf between a revolutionary who operated outside the political system and a radical-left politician who is portraying himself as a mainstream liberal working from within. Ideologically, he is bent on turning the revolutionary slogans of the 1960s into the left-liberal common sense of the 1980s. Organizationally, he wants to transform the amorphous New Left into an active political faction operating openly within the California Democratic party.

Hayden's basic political outlook has been shaped by his association with radical activists and his experiences over the years, principally during his revolutionary days as a patron saint of the New Left. The philosophy of the New Left revolved around internationalism, imperialism, militarism, and racism. Throughout the 1960s it proclaimed its soli-

darity with a variety of Marxist-Leninist revolutionaries, including Fidel Castro, Che Guevara and his Pan-American
revolution, the Uruguayan Tupamaros, the Argentinian
Montoneros, and the Viet Cong. It supported revolutionary
movements dedicated to eradicating "colonial" control exer-
cised by the United States through bilateral military agreements and multinational corporations. It denounced the
United States as a despicable and singularly exploitative society, dominated by a military-industrial complex that was
overly paranoid about communism, both in the Soviet Union
and throughout the developing countries. It depicted American international agencies as part of the plan to pillage the
Third World systematically. Finally, it vilified the United
States as racist in its treatment of internal minorities (it
viewed ghetto riots as anticolonial uprisings) and of non-
white countries and accused the United States of practicing
mass genocide on the Vietnamese because of its hunger for
oil in South Vietnam (which has never been extracted) and
because the Vietnamese were Oriental. Not only was the war
illegal, but the American political system was illegitimate.
The American economy survived because it extended capitalism into new foreign markets (the Marxist theory of imperialism). In short, "Amerika" was a sick, degenerate, and
immoral society that had to be replaced.

Hayden's present attitude toward contemporary liberalism is harshly critical. In a November 14, 1980, *Wall Street
Journal* article, he chronicled its failings:

> Motivated by the "world government" promise of
> the United Nations, liberalism became reluctant to

wave the flag too righteously, and allowed the fundamental issue of patriotic nationalism eventually to be controlled by conservatives.

Then, appalled at the "backward" Bible-thumping fundamentalists, the liberals began losing the issue of religion to the right wing. Liberalism instead became a secularized coalition of pro-abortion Catholics, moderate Protestants, Reformed Jews, Unitarians and atheists, and lately Zen Buddhists and plain mediators.

Shocked by the Vietnam War and nuclear insanity, the liberals became critics of military spending per se, without a coherent military doctrine of their own, losing the issue of national security to the likes of Richard Nixon.

Raised on the Roosevelt tradition, liberalism believed that an extension of the public sector was the answer to every ill of society. The liberals barely noticed that the unemployed of the '30s who supported Roosevelt had become the squeezed suburban taxpayers of the '70s, who supported Jarvis.

Faced with a rising wave of crime and violence, but eschewing J. Edgar Hoover's "law and order" and that of the Chicago police, the liberals acted like social psychologists as people were victimized. They seemed to counsel the citizen being stabbed to remain patient until the Humphrey-Hawkins bill passed. The conservatives began to recruit liberals who had been mugged.

Reacting to the rigid disciplinary mores of the past, liberals adopted permissiveness as a new concept of freedom. While liberals struggled to create an "alternative life style" based on "open" relationships, cocaine, Perrier and Volvos, the conservatives were busily blaming the collapse of education in the schools and productivity in the factories on Dr. Spock.[1]

This attack prompted a quick answer from journalist Nicholas Von Hoffman. After noting the charge that liberalism had lost the issues of "God, the flag, national defense, tax relief, personal safety and traditional family values to the conservatives," he cited Hayden's own culpability in this state of affairs. On losing the issue of patriotism and national defense to the conservatives, Hoffman responded acidly:

This from a man who reportedly traveled to North Vietnam and other communist countries to make statements against the United States. It was men like Mr. Hayden who made dissent, the most legitimate dissent against that unspeakable war, look like treason. Now, eight years later, this same man who babbled simple-minded, pro-communist inanities around the globe, tells the poor liberals they are the ones who handed patriotism to the conservatives . . . If liberals lost the patriotism issue it was in part because they defended Mr. Hayden's liberty to fraternize in war time with the communist enemy.[2]

Admittedly, there is some truth to Hayden's charges. Declining productivity, uncontrolled growth in many social programs, inefficient government bureaucracy, the over-regulation of business by government, large government deficits, and inflation have all been the end result of stale political and economic nostrums. Those who wish to extend the welfare state have encountered resistance from large numbers of voters. Similar criticisms have long been leveled by conservatives, who have stressed the virtues of self-reliance and self-interest in the marketplace.

What was singularly missing from the New Left rhetoric during the 1960s—directed mainly, by the way, not at conservatives but at corporate liberals and cold war liberals for supporting social programs that simply solidified the status quo—was any awareness of the left's contribution to the delegitimation of liberal idealism and the emergence of a political backlash that enabled Ronald Reagan to become president and the Moral Majority to gain prominence, at least in its own view. For his part, Hayden does not seem to recognize his own role in the decline of post–Franklin Roosevelt, New Deal liberalism. Does he believe that liberals lost confidence in the war because they had no coherent military doctrine (containment)? Wasn't it because, in some of the most prestigious and liberal universities, faculty and students joined the New Left chorus in ridiculing their doctrine and motives? Did liberals lose their confidence in governing because they were incompetent or inept (or both) or because New Left intellectuals like Hayden emphasized their illegitimacy?

The New Left perceived the loss of "system legitimacy" and the erosion of traditional values and loyalties as beneficial to itself because these processes provided at least the possibility of achieving a left-wing revolution in the United

States. Sociologist Asoke Basu has summarized the views of Richard Flacks, one of the leading New Left intellectuals, now closely associated with CED:

> Flacks argues that the American system is losing its legitimacy, as manifested by the Youth Revolt, due to the general decline of commitment to traditional "middle class values" and the erosion of the Protestant Ethic. The family itself is undergoing a transformation towards equality between the sexes, less role differentiation, and more tolerance for children. Concomitant with these changes is the rapid growth of a middle class whose status is derived from high levels of education rather than property ownership. This new middle class is more critical of traditional values, traditional capitalism, are attached to humanist values, want autonomy and a voice in decision-making, and are not structurally attached to the business sector. Flacks finds these libertarian families more resistant to authority, encourage the taking of more risks, enjoy high status and material security and pass these values on to their children.
>
> The source of discontent for this new middle class is the "persistence and growth of militarism and empire building [which] constitute a fundamental violation of central values and a severe threat to individual and collective fulfillment to central aspirations." For this class military expenditures slow domestic reform, alienates deprived minority groups, deteriorates trustworthiness, and covert operations and secrecy contribute to the

"loss of democratic control over foreign policy and an increase in direct efforts by the state to manipulate the domestic progress."[3]

In 1969, the New Left embraced permissiveness as a positive value that enabled it to challenge the system's legitimacy. It is strange that Hayden should now blame the liberals and look upon permissiveness so negatively. What is all the more remarkable about his present sentiments is that the New Left and a large number of progressive and populist social movements throughout the 1970s drew members and support from this critical, affluent, highly educated, disaffected, new middle class. Its very lack of intellectual and structural attachments to traditional values and capitalism now provides Hayden with experienced activists and volunteers and, in some measure, a core of electoral support. Could it be that the reason for Hayden's attack on liberalism lies in its dual purpose of eliminating welfare-state liberalism as a competing idea system and of hedging on his earlier views as a left-wing radical?

During his SDS and revolutionary years, Hayden's conception of legitimacy revolved around the notion of the failure of the government to live up to society's basic moral values. This is why he so regularly defamed the Johnson administration. Yet it was Hayden and the antiwar movement that were out of step with the public's attitudes toward the war and the new Nixon administration. Political analyst Ben Wattenberg, after reviewing numerous public opinion polls taken during the war, concluded that "not only did the public endorse Nixon on Vietnam, they tended to agree with him on questions of national defense." After observing that American opinion and geopolitical circumstances had changed between 1964 and 1973, Wattenberg concluded:

> Americans have resisted and rejected many move-
> ment [that is, radical] ideas. They went with Nixon,
> not McGovern, on the war. They are for some de-
> fense cuts, but will not buy major slashes seen as
> irresponsible. They do not think America's sun is
> setting. They do not think America has been a force
> of malevolence overseas. They don't buy uncondi-
> tional amnesty.[4]

Moreover, Hayden appears to have shifted his opinion about legitimacy derived from electoral victory. He regarded government officials as illegitimate because they were direct-ing a war effort that he and the antiwar movement consid-ered illegal. Since working for McGovern in 1972 and run-ning for the U.S. Senate in 1976, Hayden appears to have changed his mind. In 1975, he proclaimed that by winning elective office "we achieve the lasting legitimacy that comes from the consent of the governed."[5]

This view of legitimacy, of course, is very much a part of our political democracy. Citizens delegate to elected repre-sentatives the authority to pass laws, raise taxes, ratify treaties, and wage wars. The American system of govern-ment has not changed in these essentials for over two hun-dred years. It is still a representative democracy. What Hay-den has not clarified is why elected officials during the 1960s and 1970s were illegitimate, but his own election to office provides him with legitimacy. There are two primary roads to power in a democracy—to win an election or to be appointed to office, both of which are based on nonviolence. Hayden has turned from the violent to the electoral without ever renouncing his support of the former.

Much of Hayden's political thinking is concerned with the role of public opinion in American political life. Initially, he and the New Left emphasized the need to educate Americans about the evils of the Vietnam war. Teach-ins to raise the consciousness of faculty and students were common on college campuses. But the more public opinion and the voters supported the government, the more violent the antiwar movement became. Realizing that the "masses" would not overthrow what the radicals viewed as an illegitimate and immoral government, Hayden and others on the far left adopted the strategy of acting as the new enlightened vanguard of the revolution. Hayden's Berkeley Red Family and his admiration of the National Liberation Front in South Vietnam, the Black Panthers, and the Weather Underground reflected this revolutionary strategy.

Hayden's conversion to peaceful politics suggests that he now believes public opinion in California has moved sufficiently to the left that a former revolutionary turned progressive-liberal can be elected to office. Curiously, however, Hayden has not consistently been in the forefront of recent progressive movements in the state. Although he professed to understand the tax plight of Californians, he could not make up his mind on Proposition 13, the measure that cut the property tax burden of the suburban middle class. CED did not initiate the anti–nuclear power movement. Instead, Hayden and Jane Fonda went on a "consciousness-raising" tour *after* the anti–nuclear power movement became a national and international phenomena.

Hayden was not always opposed to nuclear power. The SDS Port Huron Statement, which he drafted, endorsed it strongly. At the time the left viewed technology favorably—in Raimondo's words, those were the "good old days when earnest young revolutionaries discussed a socialism energized by nuclear power 'too cheap to meter.'" Today, the new energy god is solar power, which Hayden wants government to promote just as it did nuclear power twenty years ago. "'Hard' technology is now 'out,' at least in certain circles, and 'soft' technology is 'in.' Now the same people who wanted a highly-centralized, high-tech, chrome-plated socialism are pushing decentralized, solar-powered (and government subsidized) 'economic democracy.'"[6]

Hayden's present strong opposition to nuclear power differs from the position of Californians as reflected in a number of polls.[7] Support for building more nuclear power plants declined from 69 percent to 41 percent in 1980. Yet, a stable majority (56–61 percent) of Californians believed that Pacific Gas and Electric's Diablo Canyon reactors should be allowed to produce electric power. Hayden has maintained a low profile on Diablo Canyon. While opposing nuclear power in general, he and CED did not participate actively in the Abalone Alliance blockades at the power plant in San Luis Obispo. This is due, in part, to the rivalry between organizations such as the CED and the Abalone Alliance, which is suspicious of most politicians and jealously guards its monopoly over this issue. Hayden's neutrality may also be explained by the support of millions of

Californians (including the labor movement) for Diablo Canyon. In contrast to his years as a practicing radical and revolutionary, he now appears more cautious about getting too far in front of public opinion.

Another example of the use of neo-Marxist myths and mirrors is Hayden's "law serves power" criticism of American society. The Marxist premise that the state is an instrument of the dominant economic class underlies Hayden's view that the U.S. government exists to serve the interests of business. He believes that the economic system is characterized by "monopoly capitalism," making the country's large corporations immune to the free market, which he has persistently treated as a rationale for an abdication of society's moral conscience. Having always claimed that big business and democracy are polar opposites, Hayden continues to see American society as polarized between corporate capitalists and the people. This simplistic anticorporatism neglects the diversity and power of organizations such as labor, trade, consumer, and environmental groups, as well as a wide range of ethnic associations. Moreover, it is a facile notion of how the federal government is organized. The growth of regulations in the 1970s could not and did not always serve the interests of corporations. It is apparent that different departments within the executive branch of government respond to different interest groups (clients or constituents). The Commerce Department is sympathetic to business problems, the Labor Department to labor problems. The Department of Energy works closely with utilities and power companies. The Environmental Protection Agency must take into consideration the views of middle-class environmental organizations. The old Health, Education and Welfare Department drew much of its support from teachers unions and welfare organizations serving the poor. In short, to conceive of business totally dominating the federal government is to misread the many sources of political power in society, as well as the nature of the state.

One other recent theme in Hayden's philosophy is xenophobia—the attempt to appeal to the lowest form of nationalism. Despite the absence of evidence that American oil companies have persistently acted to undermine the national interest, Hayden sees his mission as saving the country from their capitalist cupidity. Further, he regards American investments in foreign countries as denying Americans jobs, yet he is overly fearful of foreign investment in the United States. He apparently cannot see that rather than being a plot to control the American economy, investment by wealthy Japanese industrialists or OPEC oil merchants provides jobs in American cities and new sources of revenue for social services.

Hayden's career is more than a series of changes from student to radical to revolutionary to politician. It is intimately involved with social movements of the era. His basic strategy has been to become identified with several of them, move into the media spotlight, and promote his particular cause. He began with the civil rights movement, abandoning it when it became obvious that white, middle-class radicals were not needed or welcomed in the ghetto. Hayden and others attempted to use the antiwar movement as a vehicle for large-scale social change in American society. Although many young men flocked to antidraft rallies, some of the evidence suggests that many were attracted not for the anti-war ideology, but for a more personal reason—ending the draft. The Nixon administration's support of a volunteer army removed from the revolutionaries the one issue they had been able to use to mobilize young men. Without the draft the antiwar movement ground to a halt, despite American involvement in Vietnam until 1973. Hayden's latest tactic—the championing of solar power, environmental protection, and opposition to nuclear power—follows a similar pattern. While he did not originate any of these movements, he apparently hopes to use the rather inchoate environmental ideology that most Americans support as a basis for electoral victory.

Hayden's newest venture—a new social contract for America—revolves around recognizing the external limits to economic growth and developing "our rich inner potentials." It comes down, he says, to moving from a "wasteful, privately oriented, self-indulgent existence to a more conserving, caring and disciplined life style. The cornerstone has to be a renewal of self-reliance; not the outmoded frontier fantasy of the Republican philosophers, but the reassertion of personal responsibility in everything from conserving resources and decentralizing services to keeping ourselves well through self-care and practicing a 'right-livelihood' in business." The change he wants is "from planned obsolescence to the production of useful goods that last, from consumer madness to the achievement of inner satisfactions, from the opulence of The Great Gatsby to the frugal self-assurance of Henry David Thoreau." [8]

Hayden's new ecological philosophy holds that "these

outrages" cannot be defended any longer "by doctrines of permissiveness and consumer freedom, or by knowing shrugs of inevitability." Yet it is consumer freedom, triggered by *decontrolled* oil prices, that has helped stimulate conservative efforts and shifts in consumption patterns (particularly in automobiles) away from energy-wasting to energy-saving technologies. American consumers were not ordered to buy efficient Japanese and German autos by Hayden and CED. They simply responded to the changing international oil market in a predictable fashion. Moreover, although Hayden favors a new social order that would restrict consumer freedom, the paradox is that market economies have responded more rapidly and efficiently to the new oil market than have the command economies of the socialist bloc. The decontrol of domestic oil prices, the bane of liberals and progressives, has stimulated the desire for efficient technologies, just as the need for greater productivity and energy efficiency has generated a move toward greater use of microcomputers and silicon chips in factories and offices.

As noted earlier, Hayden has sought to transform the revolutionary rhetoric of the 1960s into the mainstream politics of the 1980s. Gone are references to American society as militarist, imperialist, and racist. Hayden now advocates environmental protection, toxic waste containment, conservation, and solar and other renewable energy sources. His new public philosophy is the latest attempt to project himself to the forefront of a new movement—in this case, environmentalism—and, of course, to propel his candidacy for elective office.

Throughout his career Hayden has demonstrated the capacity to combine and associate himself with very different ideological strains. During his tenure as a radical and revolutionary, he moved on the edges of American society as one of the most articulate and visible members of the student elite in the 1960s, an elite that saw itself as part of an adversary culture engaged in an irreconcilable clash with the bourgeois culture of those over 30. Hayden ceaselessly propagated confrontation in an attempt to promote an activist social movement. Now in search of a broader following, he wants to create a solid bloc of supporters on the liberal-left flank of the Democratic party (starting in California) who will join together in implementing his new social contract and program. Very simply, he wants to form a post-materialist electoral coalition of environmentalists, consumer protection advocates, soft-energy enthusiasts, proponents of Buddhist economics, and any other groups that feel threatened by corporate capitalism. In attempting to enlarge the social base of the New Left, he is looking for support from today's college-educated strata in society, leaving behind his old habitat of confrontationist student politics. His desire to solidify a fractured and divided left into a cohesive political force is an attempt to construct a rival not only to the materialist pro-growth emphasis on reindustrialization and rearmament shared by both labor and management but also to the better organized and financed middle-of-the-road faction in the Democratic party.

Political sociologist Seymour Martin Lipset has noted the existence of "two lefts."[9] The traditional left has historically been associated with the labor movement. It advocates economic growth, a strong defense, an anticommunist foreign policy, and conservative family values. The post-1960s New Left draws its strongest support from the college-educated middle classes and professionals. It favors a no-growth economy, reduced defense spending, an anti-anticommunist foreign policy, and a libertarian morality. It is this political left that Hayden is hoping to organize to do battle with corporate America.

After World War II the United States experienced over twenty years of economic growth and prosperity. The percentage of white-collar workers grew, and the economy began shifting from an industrial to a service-oriented economy. The country became more affluent, and the number of men and women who went to college increased. Sociologists such as Daniel Bell talked of the United States moving toward a post-industrial society. This meant, among other things, a change in values for some segments of the college-educated middle class.[10] These new beliefs are called by a variety of labels, including post-materialist values and voluntary simplicity.[11]

Central to post-materialist values is the belief in the necessity of a no-growth economy. Adherents assume, first, that there are finite limits to the amount of natural resources that can be discovered, refined, and consumed and that we are approaching these limits, particularly in fossil fuels. Second, there are limits on the ability of the natural environment to withstand the stress placed on it by an ever-expanding and consuming social environment. Failure of the biosphere would mean certain extinction of life on this planet.

In addition to this ecological ethic, post-materialism includes an "ethic of self-realization," which asserts, according to futurist Willis Harman, that "the proper end of all individual experience is the further development of the emergent self and of the human species."[12] In other words, as conventional economic growth contracts, a personal lifestyle of consuming goods and services will be replaced by psychological satisfaction and material austerity. Futurist researchers Duane S. Elgin and Arnold Mitchell point out that voluntary simplicity has historical roots "in the legendary frugality and self-reliance of the Puritans; in Thoreau's naturalistic vision at Walden Pond; in Emerson's spiritual and practical plea for 'plain living and high thinking'; in the teachings and social philosophy of a number of spiritual leaders such as Jesus and Gandhi." Its defining principle is to live in a way that is "outwardly simple and inwardly rich," embracing a process of consumption both prudent and sparing, a "strong sense of environmental urgency, a desire to return to living and working environments which are of a more human scale, and an intention to realize our higher human potential—both psychological and spiritual—in community with others."[13]

Environmental sociologist Denton E. Morrison has summarized the "challenge ideology of appropriate technology (AT)," which is a forerunner to voluntary simplicity:

> Means of production that are capital intensive, complex, large-scale, centralized, resource intensive and resource exogenous have undesirable social impacts. They displace people, especially underdogs, from jobs, alienate the employed from their work

and the unemployed from society, create overabundance for a few while depriving the masses of their basic needs or at least make them dependent on others, create social units that are vulnerable to external events, are destructive of the environment, and are ultimately destructive of the affluence they seek to create. On the other side, soft technology productive systems that involve light capital, are small in scale, decentralized, resource conserving, and resource indigenous are appropriate because they have desirable social impacts. They create meaningful work for all, supply the basic needs to all, allow self-sufficiency, and create an ecologically sustainable, higher quality of life.[14]

Morrison believes that the growing cleavage in society is between advocates of an appropriate technology and "growthists" who favor an expanding economy. Appropriate technology's most unique contribution to modern political ideology and conflict is its "substantial blurring of traditional left-right political distinctions, the blurring of traditional class conflict and the replacement of class conflict by conflict between AT advocates and all those who have their economic fate tied to more or less unrestrained economic growth via hard technology."[15]

In a similar vein, Harman notes that voluntary simplicity disputes the legitimacy of the present industrial system in three ways. First, its advocates believe that multinational corporations must be held accountable for the general welfare and that scientists cannot be arbiters of truth "because they are dominated by the values of industrialism and promote the industrial system first and human beings second." Second, they charge that there is neither an equitable distribution of the earth's resources nor "any effective ecological . . . ethic." There are no adequate goals, beyond self-interest, "to enlist the deepest loyalties and commitments of citizens." Third, they accuse the present system of failing to protect the environment, to provide satisfactory work, to ensure the welfare of future generations, and to promote "socially responsible management of the impacts of new technological applications." [16]

As for current attacks on nuclear power, they should be seen, as sociologist Robert Nisbet has observed, in the context of a "two-century history of such assaults on any and all forms of power necessary to industrialism that, while liked by the workers and consumers, was from the beginning the object of indictment by writers, artists and many philosophers—though not, be it remembered, by such progress-intoxicated prophets as Saint-Simon, Comte, and Karl Marx." [17] Biochemist H. Peter Metzger has characterized antitechnology and antigrowth movements as "coercive utopians" because their "plan is to *strangle* our society, under the guise of study and regulation, by stopping everything with which we need to grow, and that is: water, coal, and nuclear power, land use, and new industry, particularly pipelines and refineries." The end result, Metzger says, is that mandated energy shortages will create social instability and that those who oppose economic growth and technological development will attempt to gain power and manage society according to their own national agenda of planned shortages, rationing, austerity, and psychic growth. [18]

Not surprisingly, this new post-materialist worldview is found predominantly among the young, white, more affluent middle class that Hayden is trying to mobilize. The life-style does not generally appeal either to trade unionists in the industrial sector of the economy or to many ethnic minorities struggling to move out of poverty. The appeals and agenda of the post-materialists are elitist, in spite of (some would say because of) coming from those on the egalitarian left who, like Hayden, advocate participatory and economic democracy.

Their agenda is elitist in two ways. First, by curbing economic growth, they deny the poor and minorities avenues of upward social mobility through steady employment. The service sector of the economy, from which post-materialism draws the majority of its support, is oriented toward the production and manipulation of knowledge. Its base of support is found among the more highly educated and better paid. It rests upon a theory of a succession of needs that, once satisfied, produce more aesthetic needs. Thus, after needs for food, clothing, and shelter have been satisfied, new ones arise that are satisfied not by material goods, but by inner satisfaction. To the urban and rural poor, however, this theory has no meaning. They need jobs that are not keyed to high levels of education. They need such things as housing, schools for their children, and more water and electricity. Fulfilling these needs increases demand for natural resources. But the appeal of the post-materialists is that there is enough material wealth now to satisfy everyone. The real problem, they contend, is one of redistribution.

But the poor and disadvantaged have shown less interest

in the redistribution of wealth than in enjoyment of the fruits of their own labor. Having a job not only gives them an opportunity for advancement in society but provides them with a sense of self-esteem. Thus, it is not surprising that the social base of post-materialism is not found among trade unionists, the poor, and minorities.

The post-materialist agenda is elitist in a second way. At bottom, it is rooted in the belief that it is possible to plan for society's needs. Take away the chaos of the market and re-move the responsibility for investments from corporations (so that investments will be made rationally), and society will become a rationally ordered system. The trouble is that the appeal for planning and order is likely to pose a continu-ous threat to political freedom. Hayden's own agenda must be considered in the light of his wish to use and organize power to make society rational according to his own plan.

Hayden has consistently attributed the country's prob-lems to exploitation by a self-serving class of corporate rulers. These rulers will never be reduced to their proper place until society commits itself to achieving redistribution of power and greater democratization of economic and so-cial policymaking. There is more than a suggestion of the anti-urban, anti-industrial spirit of Thomas Jefferson in Hayden's attacks on the dominant economic trends of present-day society and the achievements of modernization. In keeping with the thinking of the new post-materialist left, Hayden has identified the interests of "the people" with op-position to corporate America, which, in his view, wants lit-tle more than to protect its own profits and power and the established social order.

It comes as no surprise, therefore, that among the goals of Hayden's mission is one of liberation—to free Americans from the crass materialism that constantly sacrifices the public interest to a variety of private interests engaged in selfish gain at the expense of more "humanizing" values, such as the individual's right to personal growth and self-expression. Materialism crushes the human spirit and debases the true meaning of community and equality, where citizens can feel their oneness with each other. Echoing many of the criticisms of the post-materialist left, Hayden questions some of the basic principles of modern industrial society. This is part of his attack on America's corporate economy and underscores his sympathy for the virtues of a no-growth economy where small is desirable ("I believe in free enterprise capitalism—mom-and-pop stores and family farmers") and more is not necessarily better.[19] He is also striking out at our highly impersonal and bureaucratized society, which he charges with caring more for bigness, technology, and continued economic growth than for human beings, whom it treats as cogs in the industrial machine.

As one of the leading spokesmen of the militant protest movement of the late 1960s and early 1970s, Hayden is well aware that there is no political cause on the scene today that can galvanize his followers into action in the way the Vietnam war did. Thus, he has had to direct his attention in a number of other directions. He has little interest in the current crop of young people who have turned their psychic energies inward—for example, the Me Generation that has sprung up on many campuses. This is not to suggest he would reject its support in building a new electoral coalition, but only that he regards those who have retreated into narcissism as deserting the more important cause of attacking the corporate command posts of our sociopolitical system. He draws much of his political strength from some of the post-materialist elites, including the growing number of public-interest lawyers, young professionals, civil servants, academics, and journalists—the post-industrial "new class"—who have lost faith in the present economic and political order and who participate in liberal-left political movements.

No issue better symbolizes everything Hayden has set himself against than nuclear power. As political scientist Ronald Inglehart has noted, it is the most dramatic and emotionally charged confrontation between materialist and post-materialist priorities. "One can conceive of a world in which post-materialists favored the development of nuclear power on the grounds that it disturbs the natural environment less than coal mines, petroleum wells or hydroelectric dams, and that it produces less pollution and has a better safety record than conventional energy sources. This is conceivable," he says, "but the reality is quite different."[20] Hayden's opposition to nuclear power is descended not only from his active participation in the antiwar movement but from a deep-seated distrust of big business and its influence over big government. But his antagonism also rests on his idea of the good society—or, in this case, the corrupted society. Hayden wants no part of nuclear power because (among other reasons) its complex technology was developed by large corporations and the federal government. Acting together, these two forces have led America astray by emphasizing economic growth and disregarding the environment. As part of the educated "oppositionist intelligentsia," he has a vision of a moral, decent, and democratic America based on different values and interests—and different priorities.

It is clear that Hayden shares the general outlook (if not every particular) of the post-materialists, who decry the great importance given to materialistic rather than public-interest concerns and goals. Along with the privileged, college-educated segments of the population, he is drawn to the social liberalism of the New Left and, until very recently, has shown relatively little interest in some of the issues that preoccupy the less educated, less cosmopolitan, less affluent, and less secure, such as financial and job security, a stable and enduring family, a prosperous economy, crime, and social order. His work with CED is an extension of his personal commitment and determination to restructure American society according to his current vision of the future. In the 1960s, when revolution was the watchword of the left, Hayden took to the hustings to denounce America as a malevolent power bent on economic exploitation and genocide. When the antiwar movement dissolved in the 1970s, he took up almost as his own the human potential movement, the environmental movement, and the antinuclear forces, among other causes that came to the fore. Their message was clear: America's greed is destroying the planet. Hayden has toured the country proclaiming that his program will emphasize conservation, the rational use of all types of natural and social resources, and inner spiritual growth. He has embraced the path of soft energy and small is beautiful. Underlying these new lyrics is a familiar refrain: gives us the power to change the organization of society, to make the right corporate investments, to enforce moral decisions (part of his born-again hostility towards permissiveness), and to limit consumer freedom in the marketplace. As Von Hoffman has observed, Hayden's thinking is much like that of "an authoritarian, left-wing Calvinism (advocating) a toughly supervised society over which you-know-who will prescribe and enforce the 'disciplined life style.' To the firing squad with you, Dr. Spock, you socially seditious pediatrician."[21]

When public figures such as Tom Hayden become part of the American political landscape, the media play an important role in the way they are packaged and displayed as candidates for elective office. Only on rare occasions do newspaper accounts (and television reporting virtually never) go beyond ritualistic exchanges of charges and countercharges. Time, space, and traditional practices limit the possibilities of more in-depth probing of why would-be national leaders take a particular position on major and complex political and social issues. The losers, of course, are the electorate, especially those who care enough to want to learn as much as possible about a candidate before deciding how to vote. In an article on Senator Gary Hart in the *Washington Monthly*, Robert M. Kaus, political editor for *Harper's*, stressed the need to subject candidates to serious and critical scrutiny:

> So it's worthwhile subjecting him now to what might be called the Jimmy Carter test. This test was

named for an obscure retired governor who once convinced many people, including the editors of this magazine, that he should be president. Most of them later came to regret it, as the strengths of their candidate were shown to mask fatal weaknesses.[22]

In light of Hayden's various social roles, his past and present political ideas, his often contradictory views on violence, legitimacy, morality, and freedom, as well as his economic prescriptions for the future, the real question is not "Is there a new Hayden?" That much is clear. There was a time when, as a radical and revolutionary, he frequently sounded like a sectarian inveighing against human wickedness—only his particular doctrinal issue was the incorrigible evils of the government and its leaders. Standing on the fringes of society, he drew his strength (and followers) from attacking our central political institutions and processes, which—to him—had succeeded in exploiting and deceiving the American people. Having fixed his attention on what was seen as the worst and most self-destructive features of an illegitimate social order that he had virtually washed his hands of, he found it easy in every confrontation or dispute to declare authoritatively his side absolutely right and the other totally wrong. Like the Philosopher-King, he knew the "right" ends to pursue and needed only to use the "best" means to achieve them. To extremists and true-believers who rarely miss an opportunity to turn to their own advantage every scrap of bad news that shows how badly corrupted society is, there is no long run to worry about. There is only the short run—and it is already one minute to midnight before disaster strikes. The future, if there is to be one, is expected to be grim. That is one reason why there is no time for compromise.[23] Hayden had little patience with the idea that factional conflict and the competition for power among individuals and groups in society were essential products and conditions of a political democracy. He did not understand—or, if he did, he did not care—that politics is the marketplace and the price mechanism of all social demands, with the politician often acting as the people's broker.

Now, as a politician courting the voters, he cares. He has found that in politics there is not only a short run but that everything in the short run does not look bad. There is hope. The system can work. Hayden has discovered that politics rests on disagreement, and disagreement among diverse and frequently conflicting interests, and that in a democratic system, politics is the civilizing process of conciliation. The Tom Hayden of the 1960s helped found the radical Students for a Democratic Society, led street demonstrations outside the 1968 Democratic National Convention, and shouted outside Folsom Prison to "free the leadership of the revolution" from prison. But the Tom Hayden of 1982 talked in his successful race for the California Assembly about going back to basics in education and putting more police on the streets to curb what he described as a "crisis in crime" in the 1980s. "I have more confidence in this country than I did in the past, perhaps more than most young people do," he observed. He says he has changed. "Everybody changes," he adds. He listed for the *San Jose Mercury* some of the views he has changed: he should have more quickly backed women's rights and opposed nuclear power; he should have had a "more hostile attitude" toward the Soviet Union, a lesson learned from the plight of Soviet Jews and occupied Afghanistan. He liked to show the voters in Santa Monica how far he had come from his days as a rabble-rouser by slipping into an open-collar white dress shirt with beltless, tan Movin' On jeans and jogging shoes and join several hundred walkers, joggers, and roller skaters to protest domestic violence.[24] The former street activist who for years railed against the Democratic party and the corrupt American political process is now anxious to participate in our system and to put his CED activists to work door-to-door in the precincts to get out the vote for Democrats. Today he is inviting the support of Democratic leaders, not fighting them. In adapting his ideas to the realities of what a candidate must do to win, he raised and spent (with wife Jane's help) over $1 million to join the Establishment as a politician and an elected leader of the Democrats.

For their part, leaders in the California Democratic party are keeping a cautious eye on Hayden. While many feel they need him, many others do not trust him. Yet they recognize that he is a skilled and cunning politician who has put together an impressive and efficient organization that Chicago's Mayor Richard Daley would have appreciated. He is the only person in the state who can turn out at the polls thousands of left-liberals who will support the kind of Democrat—former Governor Jerry Brown is a good example—who has a constituency on the left and who works assiduously to protect himself from attacks and defections.

Hayden's major problem, however, is the precise opposite. Much of his basic political appeal is to upper middle-class liberal-to-radical voters (affluent and highly educated) and (on local issues like rent control) to the elderly. As a longtime Democratic leader in southern California privately observed, "Hayden is pretty much anathema to the blacks and Mexican-Americans. Labor has never liked him. Many Jews don't trust him and think his present interest in Israel is cynical and suitable to his electoral ambitions. So his strategy now is to broaden his support. He is not above making closed-door approaches to business—or to any one else. All you really need to know about Hayden," he says, "is that he is a thorough opportunist [Gore Vidal is said to have remarked that Hayden 'is starting to give opportunism a bad name.'] who would dump any of his supporters if it would help him get what he wants. And what he wants right now is to get closer to the mainstream of Democratic politics in California."

If this judgment seems bitter, it is because he speaks for many Democrats who have watched and listened to Hayden over the years and have not forgotten his attacks on liberals, labor, and others whose political backing he sought in his recent political campaign and will continue to cultivate. He is regarded with suspicion and apprehension by so many people (and by some as a danger) because of his reputation for being able to rise above principle when it serves his immediate purposes. Not too many years ago he was a major spokesman for a radical movement that stressed the need for violence to organize its ranks and to capture people's minds. Today Hayden claims that the moribund, decadent system he once reviled he now wants to save. How? Not by the constant process of confrontation that he once advocated, but by acquiring the political power and influence to achieve Economic Democracy and prevent America from dooming itself.

As he looks down the road at the long run, Hayden wants to replace the present-day profit ethic with the "quality of life" ethic. As he sees it, the primary challenge is to make our economic and political institutions more accountable and participatory, to elect the right people to office, to organize the unorganized workers at their work place (especially women, clerical workers, and so on), and to build up a network of neighborhood groups to fight against corporate power and city hall. Hayden doubts that America can continue to rely on its past history of an open frontier and expanding resources to accommodate the pressures of social revolution. He sees a new era in which the possibilities of expansion may simply be gone, perhaps leading to the dissolution of the marriage of liberal democracy and corporate capitalism, a marriage he has frequently felt was based more on uncontrolled greed than moral principle. Not too many years ago, he had little difficulty in foreseeing the future. Today he is less certain. Nonetheless, he believes that only minimal rather than real change in our society is likely to be achieved because many of the fundamental inequities—such underlying problems as powerlessness and alienation—do not get addressed by American reformers. Thus for Hayden the task ahead appears no less radical than the task of the 1960s.[25]

No one can doubt that there is a new Hayden. What remains to be seen is whether the new Tom Hayden is the real Tom Hayden.

notes

preface

1. Tom Hayden, "An 'Activist' Agenda for Liberals," *Wall Street Journal*, November 14, 1980, p. 30. See also Tom Hayden, "The Future Politics of Liberalism," *The Nation*, February 21, 1981, p. 210.

2. John C. Boland, "Anti-Capitalist Roadshow: Jane Fonda, Tom Hayden Lead a Cast of Thousands," *Barron's*, October 29, 1979, p. 5.

chapter 1

1. Milton Viorst, *Fire in the Streets* (New York: Simon & Schuster, 1979), pp. 93–124.

2. Ibid., p. 166.

3. Tim Findley, "Tom Hayden: *Rolling Stone* Interview, Part 1," *Rolling Stone*, October 26, 1972, p. 38.

4. Ibid.

5. Ibid.

6. Viorst, *Fire in the Streets*, pp. 172–73.

7. Findley, "Tom Hayden," p. 38.

8. Kirkpatrick Sale, *SDS* (New York: Random House, 1973), pp. 16–17. Much of the material on SDS in this paper is taken from Sale's book.

9. Davis later became one of Hayden's codefendants in the Chicago 7 trial following student and police rioting during the 1968 Democratic National Convention in Chicago.

10. It was later discovered that the NSA was supported by the CIA. Although the agency rarely interfered with the NSA's domestic programs, it held tight rein on its international activities. Hayden later attributed his lack of success in the NSA to CIA influence.

11. Viorst, *Fire in the Streets*, pp. 178–79.

12. Sale, *SDS*, p. 35.

13. Students for a Democratic Society, "The Port Huron Statement," in Massimo Teodori, ed., *The New Left: A Documentary History* (Indianapolis and New York: Bobbs-Merrill, 1969), p. 164.

14. Findley, "Tom Hayden," p. 44.

15. Ibid., p. 46.

16. Ibid., p. 48.

17. Staughton Lynd and Thomas Hayden, *The Other Side* (New York: New American Library, 1966).

18. Jack Newfield, "Tom Hayden: Prophet Comes to Sodom," *Village Voice*, January 20, 1966, p. 25. Actually, the State Depart-

ment later suspended all three travelers' passports until the following year.

19. Sale, *SDS*, p. 145.

20. Ibid., p. 149.

21. Findley, "Tom Hayden," p. 46.

22. Steven V. Roberts, "Will Tom Hayden Overcome?" *Esquire*, December 1968, p. 176.

23. Tom Hayden, *Trial* (New York: Holt, Rinehart & Winston, 1970), p. 108.

24. Peter Collier, "I Remember Fonda," *New West*, September 24, 1979, p. 22.

25. The other four convicted were Rennie Davis, a colleague of Hayden's from the beginning of SDS and a co-coordinator of the National Mobilization in Chicago; Dave Dellinger, a lifelong pacifist who had served with the Red Cross during the Spanish Civil War, had been jailed on draft evasion charges during World War II, and was a co-coordinator of the Mobilization; and Yippie leaders Abbie Hoffman and Jerry Rubin. The other two defendants, activists John Froines and Lee Weiner, were acquitted on all counts except contempt. In addition, Black Panther chairman Bobby Seale originally was indicted with the other seven, but Judge Julius Hoffman declared a mistrial in his case. He was not recharged, although he was sentenced to over four years in jail for contempt. The defense attorneys, Leonard Weinglass and William Kunstler, were also given lengthy sentences for contempt.

26. "Chicago Case Overturned," *Facts on File*, November 25, 1972, p. 930.

27. Collier, "I Remember Fonda," p. 23.

28. Ibid.

29. Tim Findley, "Tom Hayden: *Rolling Stone* Interview, Part

2," *Rolling Stone*, November 9, 1972, p. 29. Weather was one of three factions that emerged from the destruction of SDS at the end of 1968. Members referred to themselves first as Weathermen, later as the nonsexist Weatherpeople, and finally as the Weather Underground. They envisioned themselves as a communist cadre whose task was to disrupt the country by any possible means. Weather probably was the most violent of the white revolutionary organizations. Members lived in rigidly disciplined collectives and tried to spur the masses to revolution. Their most famous action was the November 1969 Days of Rage in Chicago, where they battled with police and indiscriminately battered automobiles, homes, and unfortunate passersby. Other favorite tactics were bombing government buildings and invading high schools to "liberate" students.

30. Collier, "I Remember Fonda," p. 23. Also Dave Dellinger, *More Power Than We Know: The People's Movement Toward Democracy* (Garden City, N.Y.: Doubleday, Anchor Press, 1975), p. 130. What appears to be an indirect reference to the school may be found in Frank Bardacke and Tom Hayden, "Free Berkeley," in Matthew Stolz, ed., *Politics of the New Left* (Beverly Hills, Calif.: Glencoe Press, 1971), p. 152.

31. Joel Kotkin, "Tom Hayden's Manifest Destiny," *Esquire*, May 1980, p. 44.

32. Collier, "I Remember Fonda," p. 23.

33. Kotkin, "Tom Hayden's Manifest Destiny," p. 44.

34. Tom Hayden, "How to Vote for the Vietnamese," *Ramparts*, October 1972, p. 44.

35. Collier, "I Remember Fonda," pp. 20–22. The trip earned her the nickname "Hanoi Jane." She had spoken over Radio Hanoi against U.S. bombing in the North and overall U.S involvement in the war. One notorious photograph showed her posing in the seat of a North Vietnamese antiaircraft gun. Newspapers around the

country called for her indictment on charges of treason and a boy-cott of her movies.

36. *Playboy* Interview: Jane Fonda and Tom Hayden," *Playboy*, April 1974, p. 184.

37. Ibid., p. 180.

38. Kotkin, "Tom Hayden's Manifest Destiny," p. 48.

39. Collier, "I Remember Fonda," p. 20.

40. Kotkin, "Tom Hayden's Manifest Destiny," p. 48.

41. Tom Hayden, "A Conversation with Jimmy Carter," *CED News*, February 1978, p. 7.

42. W. E. Barnes, "A Hard Look: Hayden's Power Base Grows," *San Francisco Examiner & Chronicle*, July 12, 1981, p. A8.

43. Kotkin, "Tom Hayden's Manifest Destiny," p. 52.

44. Tom Hayden, "What of the Radical Left of the 1960s?" *Current*, November 1978, p. 10.

45. Barnes, "A Hard Look," p. A8.

46. Kotkin, "Tom Hayden's Manifest Destiny," p. 51.

chapter 2

1. *Meet the Press* interview with Tom Hayden and Jane Fonda, September 23, 1979. Transcript published by Kelly Press, Washington, D.C., p. 6.

2. Herbert Gans, *More Equality* (New York: Pantheon, 1968), pp. 66–67.

3. Tom Hayden, "The Ability to Face Whatever Comes," *New Republic*, January 15, 1966, p. 16.

4. Students for a Democratic Society, "The Port Huron State-ment," in Massimo Teodori, ed., *The New Left: A Documen-*

tary History (Indianapolis and New York: Bobbs-Merrill, 1969), p. 164.

5. Ibid.

6. Tom Hayden, "Who Are the Student Boat-Rockers?" *Mademoiselle*, August 1961, p. 42.

7. Jack Newfield, *A Prophetic Minority* (New York: New American Library, 1966), p. 142.

8. Staughton Lynd and Thomas Hayden, *The Other Side* (New York: New American Library, 1966), p. 225.

9. Tom Hayden, *Rebellion and Repression* (New York and Cleveland: World Publishing, 1969), p. 26.

10. Ibid., pp. 24–25.

11. Ibid., p. 24.

12. "Confrontation: The Old Left and the New," *American Scholar*, Autumn 1967, p. 569.

13. Hayden, *Rebellion and Repression*, p. 30.

14. Tom Hayden, *Trial* (New York: Holt, Rinehart & Winston, 1970), pp. 126–27.

15. The current version of this strategy is the CED tactic of building support by recruiting local activists around issues such as rent control.

16. "Confrontation," p. 586.

17. Hayden, *Trial*, pp. 160–64.

18. Tom Hayden, *Rebellion in Newark: Official Violence and Ghetto Response* (New York: Random House, 1967), pp. 70–71.

19. Richard Parker, "Radical Soap Opera," *New Republic*, November 17, 1979, p. 22.

20. Lawrence Lader, *Power on the Left: American Radical Movements Since 1946* (New York: W. W. Norton & Co., 1979), p. 248.

21. Tom Hayden, "Two, Three, Many Columbias," *Ramparts*, June 15, 1968, p. 40.

22. Frank Bardacke and Tom Hayden, "Free Berkeley," in Matthew Stolz, ed., *Politics of the New Left* (Beverly Hills, Calif.: Glencoe Press, 1971), pp. 142–43.

23. Peter Collier, "I Remember Fonda," *New West*, September 24, 1979, p. 23.

24. Carl Johnston, "Hayden Looks Back at Activism Years' sic," *Stanford Daily*, March 7, 1980, p. 3; and *Meet the Press* interview, p. 3.

25. Tom Hayden, "The Battle for Survival," in Peter Babcox, Deborah Babcox, and Bob Axel, eds., *The Conspiracy* (New York: Dell, 1969), p. 168. Hayden expressed the same sentiment in *Rebellion and Repression*, p. 13.

26. Hayden, "Battle for Survival," p. 168.

27. Hayden, *Rebellion and Repression*, p. 72.

28. Ibid.

29. Dave Dellinger, *More Power Than We Know: The People's Movement Toward Democracy* (Garden City, N.Y.: Doubleday, Anchor Press, 1975), pp. 168–69.

30. Hayden, *Rebellion and Repression*, p. 75.

31. Ibid., p. 183.

32. Thomas Hayden, "Student Social Action: From Liberation to Community," in Mitchell Cohen and Dennis Hale, eds., *The New Student Left* (Boston: Beacon Press, 1966), p. 285.

33. Hayden, "Two, Three, Many Columbias," p. 40.

34. SDS, "Port Huron Statement," p. 172.

35. Sidney Hook, *Academic Freedom and Academic Anarchy* (New York: Cowles, 1969–1970), p. 56.

36. Hayden, *Rebellion and Repression*, p. 43.

37. Tim Findley, "Tom Hayden: *Rolling Stone* Interview, Part 1," *Rolling Stone*, October 26, 1972, p. 50.

38. Johnston, "Hayden Looks Back," p. 3.

39. "*Playboy* Interview: Jane Fonda and Tom Hayden," *Playboy*, April 1974, p. 70.

40. Tim Findley, "Tom Hayden: *Rolling Stone* Interview, Part 2," *Rolling Stone*, November 9, 1972, p. 29.

41. Tom Hayden, *The American Future: New Visions Beyond Old Frontiers* (Boston: South End Press, 1980), p. 154.

42. Ibid., p. 23.

43. *Spotlight* interview with Tom Hayden, broadcast on KZSU radio, Stanford, Calif., January 21, 1981.

44. Hayden, *The American Future*, pp. 27–28.

45. Ibid., p. 198.

46. Ibid., p. 15.

47. Ibid., pp. 33–39, 310.

chapter 3

1. Tom Hayden, "The Future Politics of Liberalism," *The Nation*, February 21, 1981, p. 212.

2. W. E. Barnes, "A Hard Look: Hayden's Power Base Grows," *San Francisco Examiner & Chronicle*, July 12, 1981, p. A8.

3. Ibid.

4. Quoted in the *Chico* (Calif.) *Enterprise-Record*, May 18, 1981.

5. Quoted in Justin Raimondo, "Inside the CED," *Reason*, February 1982, p. 19. Raimondo is editor of the *Libertarian Vanguard*.

6. *Berkeley Barb*, October 4–17, 1979.

7. Raimondo, "Inside the CED," p. 18.

8. Lee Fremstad and Thomas D. Elias, "Tom Hayden Blends Old, New Politics," *Sacramento Bee*, May 31, 1981, p. A12.

9. Ibid., p. A13.

10. Bob Baker, "Court Hits Tough Rent Control Law," *Los Angeles Times*, March 10, 1981, p. 1.

11. Peter Marcuse's "The Strategic Potential of Rent Control," which is reprinted in *The Political Economy of Rent Control: Theory and Strategy*, Papers in Planning no. 7 (New York: Columbia University, Division of Urban Planning, 1979), is a candid and perceptive discussion of the role rent control will (and will not) play in "future struggles for progressive social change."

12. John Judis, "Perhaps a Great Notion," *In These Times*, May 9–15, 1979, p. 14.

13. Derek Shearer, quoted in Raimondo, "Inside the CED," p. 20.

14. John C. Boland, "Nader Crusade: The Anti-Business Lobby Is Alive and Kicking," *Barron's*, October 12, 1981, p. 20.

15. Ibid.

16. Quoted in "Speaking Openly of Honesty" (editorial), *Santa Monica Evening Outlook*, p. B1.

17. *60 Minutes* segment called "Left City," March 14, 1982. The president of the Santa Monica Chamber of Commerce, Bob Gabriel, says that if the "redistribution of wealth isn't socialism, then I don't know what the hell is" (quoted in Lawrence V. Cott, "What the New Left Has Done to Santa Monica," *Human Events*, April 17, 1982, p. 333). But Mayor Goldway said on *60 Minutes*, "It's not a question of redistributing the wealth as much as it is equalizing the equation here."

18. Eric Mankin, "You CAN Win City Hall," *Mother Jones*, December 1981, p. 66.

19. Quoted in Fremstad and Elias, "Tom Hayden," p. A13.

20. Ibid.

21. Eleanor Randolph, "Liberals Are Embracing the States' Rights Movement," *San Francisco Chronicle*, April 22, 1981, p. C-7.

22. For an excellent historical account of the "two traditions of American political thought that grew out of a quarrel at the time of the Founding in 1787," see William A. Schambra, "The Roots of American Public Philosophy," *Public Interest*, no. 67 (Spring 1982): 36–48.

23. *60 Minutes*, March 14, 1982.

chapter 4

1. Tom Hayden, *The American Future: New Visions Beyond Old Frontiers* (Boston: South End Press, 1980), pp. 162–63.

2. Tom Hayden, *Make the Future Ours* (Santa Monica, Calif.: Tom Hayden for U.S. Senate Campaign, 1976), p. 46.

3. John C. Boland, "Anti-Capitalist Roadshow: Jane Fonda, Tom Hayden Lead a Cast of Thousands," *Barron's*, October 29, 1979, p. 4.

4. Hayden, *The American Future*, p. 155. The largest oil company controls only one-twelfth of the market, which means that "four or five firms" could not control, as Hayden charges, more than half the oil market (see Robert Hessen, *In Defense of the Corporation* [Stanford: Hoover Institution Press, 1979], p. 93).

5. *Meet the Press* interview with Tom Hayden and Jane Fonda, September 23, 1979. Transcript published by Kelly Press, Washington, D.C., p. 1.

6. Hayden, *The American Future*, p. 195.

7. Ralph Nader, Mark Green, and Joel Seligman, *Taming the*

Giant Corporation (New York: W. W. Norton & Co., 1976), p. 81.

8. Hayden, *The American Future*, pp. 156–57.

9. Ibid., pp. 156, 168–69.

10. Francis W. Steckmest, *Corporate Performance* (New York: McGraw-Hill, 1982), pp. 11–12.

11. Robert L. Simison, "UAW and Foreign Unions Plan Strategies to Confront World-Wide Firms Like GM," *Wall Street Journal*, June 24, 1981, p. 45.

12. Neil Jacoby, *Corporate Power and Social Responsibility: A Blueprint for the Future* (New York: Macmillan, 1973), p. 153. See also p. 155.

13. Eugene Bardach, "Pluralism Reconsidered," in Robert Hessen, ed., *Does Big Business Rule America?* (Washington, D.C.: Ethics and Public Policy Center, 1981), p. 15.

14. Jacoby, *Corporate Power*, p. 157.

15. Ibid.

16. Ithiel de Sola Pool, "How Powerful Is Business?" in Hessen, *Does Big Business Rule America?*, pp. 33–34.

17. James Q. Wilson, "Democracy and the Corporation," in Hessen, *Does Big Business Rule America?*, p. 37.

18. *Meet the Press* interview, p. 1.

19. Robert A. Dahl, *After the Revolution? Authority in a Good Society* (New Haven, Conn.: Yale University Press, 1970), pp. 64–67.

20. Hayden, *The American Future*, p. 203.

21. Hayden, *Make the Future Ours*, p. 46.

22. Hessen, *In Defense of the Corporation*, p. 96.

23. Hayden, *Make the Future Ours*, p. 46.

24. Robert E. Lane, *Political Ideology: Why the American*

Common Man Believes What He Does (New York: Free Press of Glencoe, 1962), pp. 61, 68–71, 250–51.

25. J. R. Pole, *The Pursuit of Equality in American History* (Berkeley and Los Angeles: University of California Press, 1978), p. 351.

26. Boland, "Anti-Capitalist Roadshow," p. 23.

27. Hayden, *The American Future*, pp. 54, 93.

28. Ibid., p. 199*n*.

29. "*Playboy* Interview: Jane Fonda and Tom Hayden," *Playboy*, April 1974, p. 184.

30. *Meet the Press* interview, pp. 1, 3–4.

31. Hayden, *The American Future*, pp. 110, 179–80, 182.

32. Boland, "Anti-Capitalist Roadshow," p. 5.

33. Justin Raimondo, "Inside the CED," *Reason*, February 1982, p. 23.

34. Ibid.

35. Hayden, *The American Future*, p. 186; and Mark Green and Robert Massie, Jr., eds., *Big Business Reader* (New York: Pilgrim Press, 1980), p. 591, quoted in Hayden, *The American Future*, p. 188.

36. Tom Hayden, "An 'Activist' Agenda for Liberals," *Wall Street Journal*, November 14, 1980, p. 30.

37. Hayden, *The American Future*, pp. 55, 57; Boland, "Anti-Capitalist Roadshow," p. 5; and Tom Hayden, "The Crisis of Liberalism," *CED News*, April 1979, p. 6.

38. For a fuller discussion of state and municipal pension funds as attractive sources of "alternative financing," see Cameron La Follette, "Public Pension Funds Being Channeled into Local Economic Development," *National Journal*, August 21, 1982, pp. 1466–469.

39. Tom Hayden, "The Ability to Face Whatever Comes," *New Republic*, January 15, 1966, p. 17.

40. John Judis, "Perhaps a Great Notion," *In These Times*, May 9–15, 1979, p. 14.

41. Tom Hayden, "What of the Radical Left of the 1960s?" *Current*, November 1978, p. 9.

42. Hayden, *The American Future*, p. 177.

43. Ibid., pp. 246–49.

44. Ibid., pp. 157–58.

45. Ibid., pp. 98, 162, 171; and Tom Hayden, "The Future Politics of Liberalism," *The Nation*, February 21, 1981, p. 210.

46. Hayden, "The Crisis of Liberalism," p. 3; idem, *The American Future*, pp. 43–46; idem, "The Future Politics," p. 209; and idem, *Make the Future Ours*, p. 74.

47. Hayden, "The Crisis of Liberalism," p. 4.

48. Hayden, *The American Future*, pp. 61–69, 159–60, 171.

49. Harold Keen, "The Strategy of Tom Hayden," *San Diego Magazine*, June 1980, pp. 238–39.

50. *Meet the Press* interview, p. 2.

51. Hayden, *The American Future*, p. 100.

52. Ibid., p. 92.

53. Ibid., p. 98.

54. Ibid., p. 170.

55. Ibid., p. 197.

56. "It was the largest single organized force on the California Left, and, unlike other New Left groups that chose their issues only after long wrangling among the members, CED was run like a family business. Its books were closed to the public, its fund raising and decision-making rested almost totally with Tom and his aides."

(Joel Kotkin, "Tom Hayden's Manifest Destiny," *Esquire*, May 1980, p. 48.)

57. Boland, "Anti-Capitalist Roadshow," p. 5.

58. Kotkin, "Tom Hayden's Manifest Destiny," p. 51.

59. Seymour Martin Lipset, "Social Mobility in Industrial Societies," *Public Opinion* 5, no. 3 (June/July 1982): 42.

chapter 5

1. Tom Hayden, "An 'Activist' Agenda for Liberals," *Wall Street Journal*, November 14, 1980, p. 30.

2. Nicholas Von Hoffman, "Tom Hayden's Liberal Manifesto," *Rocky Mountain News*, December 3, 1980, p. 55.

3. Asoke Basu, *Culture, Politics, and Critical Academics* (Sadar, India: Archana Publications, 1981), pp. 70–71.

4. Ben J. Wattenberg, *In Search of the Real America* (New York: G. P. Putnam, 1976), pp. 208, 211.

5. Tom Hayden, "Foreword: A Chance to Win," *Working Papers for a New Society* 3, no. 3 (March/April 1978): 15.

6. Justin Raimondo, "The CED Syndrome: The Politics of the New Class," *Libertarian Review*, January 1980, p. 20.

7. California Opinion Index, "Energy," vol. 7 (San Francisco: Field Institute, 1980).

8. Hayden, "An 'Activist' Agenda for Liberals," p. 30.

9. Seymour Martin Lipset, "Whatever Happened to the Proletariat?" in Jan Triska and C. Gati, eds., *Blue Collar Workers in Eastern Europe* (London: Allen & Unwin, 1981), pp. 14–15.

10. Daniel Bell, *The Coming of Post-Industrial Society* (New York: Basic Books, 1973).

11. Ronald Inglehart, *The Silent Revolution* (Princeton, N.J.:

Princeton University Press, 1977), p. 28; and Duane S. Elgin and Arnold Mitchell, "Voluntary Simplicity: Lifestyle of the Future," *The Futurist* 11, no. 4 (August 1977): 200–206, 208–9.

12. Willis W. Harman, "The Coming Transformation," *The Futurist* 11, no. 2 (August 1977): 106–12.

13. Elgin and Mitchell, "Voluntary Simplicity," pp. 200–201.

14. Denton E. Morrison, "Energy, Appropriate Technology, and International Interdependence" (Paper delivered at a meeting of the Society for the Study of Social Problems, San Francisco, August 1978), pp. 7–8.

15. Ibid., pp. 33–34.

16. Harman, "The Coming Transformation," p. 107.

17. Robert Nisbet, "The Rape of Progress," *Public Opinion* 2, no. 3 (June/July 1979): 4.

18. H. Peter Metzger, *The Coercive Utopians: Their Hidden Agenda*, Public Service Company of Colorado Pamphlet (Denver, 1979), p. 14.

19. Tom Hayden, *San Francisco Chronicle*, August 27, 1979.

20. Ronald Inglehart, "Post-Materialism in an Environment of Insecurity," *American Political Science Review* 75 (1981): 896. There can be little doubt that post-industrial politics is increasingly concerned with noneconomic issues, as Lipset and others have pointed out. However, the issue of a clean environment cannot be classified as simple post-materialism. Unlike many of the new social, cultural, and life-style issues that are distinguishable from economic or "materialist" goals, environmental protection has strong backing from all educational, occupational, and income groups in the United States. As Everett C. Ladd has noted, during the 1960s and 1970s Americans in all social and economic positions "came to include such objectives as cleaner water and air as among those they wanted to 'buy.' Environmental concerns, at the mass pub-

lic level, were not 'post-materialist'; rather, they were a later-generation material emphasis." In short, large majorities of the people "have come to feel that clean rivers and clean air are something they have a basic claim to—not as an exotic new cultural expression but as plain garden-variety materialism." Americans have always wanted "more." The meaning of "more" has changed throughout our history with economic development, observes Ladd. "And today it includes a clean and healthy environment just as securely as it does good housing, motor cars, vacations, and television sets." (Ladd, "Clearing the Air: Public Opinion and Public Policy on the Environment," *Public Opinion*, February/March 1982, pp. 18–19.)

21. Von Hoffman, "Tom Hayden's Liberal Manifesto," p. 55.

22. Robert M. Kaus, "Should Gary Hart Be President?" *Washington Monthly* 13, no. 8 (October 1981): 33.

23. For a perceptive analysis of the concepts of "center" and "border" in politics, see Mary Douglas and Aaron Wildavsky, *Risk and Culture* (Berkeley and Los Angeles: University of California Press, 1982), pp. 83–125.

24. Dan Meyers, "Tom Hayden Turns to TV to Counter Radical Change," *San Jose Mercury*, October 19, 1982, p. 1.

25. Irving Howe, a longtime socialist and member of the Old Left, remembers Tom Hayden well. He first met him in 1962, when several members of the new Students for a Democratic Society visited the editorial board of *Dissent*, the magazine that Howe edited. As many others have frequently observed, Hayden was "the most brilliant among them." But Howe was disturbed by other qualities in Hayden that have also been noted by many who have known or observed him—"the most rigid, perhaps even fanatical," says Howe. Howe had more to say:

> Pinched in manner, holding in some obscure personal rage,
> he spoke as if he were already an experienced, canny "po-

litical"; after the meeting, a number of Dissenters remarked spontaneously that in Hayden's clenched style—
that air of distance suggesting reserves of power—one
could already see the beginnings of a commissar. All
through the 60's I kept encountering Hayden, each time
impressed by his gifts yet also persuaded that the authoritarian poisons of this century had seeped into the depths
of his mind.

(Irving Howe, "The Decade That Failed," *New York Times Magazine*, September 1982, p. 43.)